Texas Assessment Preparation

Grade 3

TEXAS
JOURNEYS

TEXAS
WRITE
SOURCE

 HOUGHTON MIFFLIN HARCOURT

Excerpt from "Listen, Rabbit!" by Aileen Fisher. Text copyright © 1964 by Aileen Fisher. Reprinted by permission of Marian Reiner Literary Agency on behalf of the author.

Excerpt from "Mrs. McRitter's Cricket" by Heather A. Meloche from *Spider Magazine*, Volume 13, Number 9, September 2006. Text copyright © 2006 by Heather Meloche. Reprinted by permission of Carus Publishing Company.

Excerpt from *Snowflake Bentley* by Jacqueline Briggs Martin. Text copyright © 1998 by Jacqueline Briggs Martin. Reprinted by permission of Houghton Mifflin Harcourt Publishing Company.

Excerpt from "Up, Down, and Turned Around" from *Click Magazine*, July/August 2010, Vol. 13, No. 6. Text copyright © 2010 by Carus Publishing Company. Reprinted by permission of Cricket Magazine Group, Carus Publishing Company.

Excerpt from *Wind* by Nate LeBoutillier. Text copyright © 2007 by Creative Education. Reprinted by permission of Creative Education, an imprint of The Creative Company.

ISBN 978-0-547-74906-8

6 7 8 9 10   0928   20 19 18 17 16 15 14 13

4500414262   A B C D E F G

Contents

How To Use This Book

This book will help you practice for the Texas reading and writing tests. The book is in four parts: Reading, Writing, Revising, and Editing.

- **Reading**   This part includes passages in different genres. A **genre** is a type of literature, such as fiction, expository nonfiction, or poetry. Helpful **Tips** guide you as you read the passages and answer the questions about them.

- **Writing**   This part has writing prompts that will tell you which topic to write about. There are also samples of other student's writing to show you what to do (and not do) in order to write well.

- **Revising and Editing**   These parts help you practice ways to improve your writing before you create a final draft.

Get Credit for Your Answers

- **Multiple-Choice Questions**   On your test page, fill in each correct answer bubble completely. Check your work. Be sure you have not missed a question or filled in more than one bubble for a question.

- **Writing Prompts**   You may use your own paper when you start to write. You can use this first draft to make all of your changes. When you write your final draft, write as clearly as possible. Be sure that your final draft is no more than one page long.

Read the Signs

As you work through this book, you will see the signs and symbols below. Be sure you understand what they mean and what to do when you see them.

Read this selection.	Words in a box give directions. Read them carefully to make sure you understand what to do.
In paragraph 10, the word <u>genre</u> means —	Look carefully for underlined words in a passage. These words will appear later in questions about the passage.
What is the **BEST** way to revise sentence 7?	Words like **BEST** are clues to help you think about how to decide which answer is correct.
GO ON ▶	When you see this arrow, you should go on to the next page.
STOP	When you see this stop sign, you should put your pencil down.

Texas Assessment Practice

Fiction

Genre Overview

Fiction refers to a story that is made up. In every fiction story, there is at least one **character**, at least one **setting**, and a **plot**. These parts work together in the **story structure**.

As you read a fiction story, identify the **characters**. Notice how the characters act towards one another. Pay attention to what they think, do, and say. Ask yourself how a character changes in the story.

The **setting** is the place and time in which the story happens. To identify the setting, ask yourself, "Where and when does this story take place?"

The **plot** is what happens in a story. The plot is made up of a series of events. The **problem** is usually introduced near the beginning of the story. The **solution**, how the problem is solved, comes towards the end of the story. The **theme** refers to the message that the author wants to send to the reader.

The **narrator** is the person who tells a story. When a character tells the story, he or she is called a **first-person** narrator. A first-person narrator uses words such as *I* and *we* to tell the story. When the narrator is not a character in the story, he or she is called a **third-person** narrator. A third-person narrator tells the story using words such as *he, she, it,* and *they*.

Sometimes an author will provide details that clearly explain his or her main points. Sometimes the reader needs to tie details together to **infer**, or figure out, what the author does not state directly.

As you read, you may need to figure out the meaning of unfamiliar words. Word parts at the beginning and end of words can help you. A **prefix** is a word part added to the beginning of a base word or root word. A **suffix** is a word part added to the end of a base word or root word. Each prefix or suffix changes the meaning of the root word or base word. For example, the prefix *dis-* means "not." So the word *dislike* means "not like." The suffix *-y* means "full of," so the word *rusty* means "full of rust."

Name _____ Date _____

Fiction

> **Read this selection. Then answer the questions that follow it.**
> **Fill in the circle of the correct answer.**

Big Brother and the Bats

1   Clara was excited to visit her brother in Austin. Andrew may have been ten years older than Clara, but she still thought of him as her best friend. She had missed him terribly since he had moved away to attend the University of Texas. So far, she only saw him when he visited on weekends. Now her parents were taking her to Austin. As the family car pulled up to Andrew's new home, Clara was thrilled.

2   "Hey, Squirt!" Andrew called as Clara ran to meet him at the front of his building. "Welcome to Austin! I have lots of fun stuff planned. We're going to hear some music, and then eat lunch by the river, and don't forget the bats—"

3   *Oh no,* Clara thought. Andrew had said that he wanted to take her to see the famous Congress Street Bridge bats, but she had hoped he'd forget about it. Just the thought of one creepy bat flying at her head made her want to jump back into the car.

4   "I don't really love bats," Clara said, trying to hide her worry.

5   "Aww, a few bats won't hurt you," Dad said. "Besides, it's amazing to see. Just as the sun goes down, the bats fly out from under the Congress Street Bridge. They look beautiful against the colorful sky."

> **Tip**
>
> Think about what Clara and Andrew think, say, and do. What do these clues tell you about the relationship between Clara and Andrew?

GO ON

Grade 3: Fiction

Fiction

TEKS 3.4A, 3.5A, 3.8A, 3.8B, RC-3(D), RC-3(E)

6   "Dad's right," Andrew said with a smile. "It's awesome. Though we're not talking about a *few* bats. More like a million!" Clara gulped.

7   Clara tried all afternoon not to think of the bats. She tried not to think of them as Andrew introduced her to his new friends. She tried not to think of them as she munched on a barbecued turkey sandwich. She tried not to think of them as the sun fell lower and lower in the sky.

8   Fortunately, Andrew knew his little sister. "You're really freaked out, aren't you?" he asked as the family walked through the park where they planned to watch the bats. Clara nodded.

9   "Well, I'll tell you what. We don't have to get too close. We'll stay here under this tree and watch them from here!"

10   Clara was relieved. She could see the bridge, but it was far away. Surely the bats could not get to her from that distance. Then, as she sat down and watched the sky turn pink over the bridge, she saw them.

11   First, she just saw a few. Then she saw a few more. Before she knew it, what seemed like a hundred million bats were flying out from under the bridge in every direction. She'd never seen so many bats before! Dad was right, it really was amazing. Her jaw dropped.

12   Andrew gave her a squeeze. "What do you think, Squirt?"

13   "Well, I still don't like bats," Clara said, hugging him back. "But I'm always happy to see *you*!"

Tip

Stop every few paragraphs to think about what has happened so far. Think about what might happen next.

Tip

Think about how Andrew helps Clara get over her fear. Use this clue to help you figure out the theme of the selection.

GO ON ➡

1 In paragraph 5, the word <u>colorful</u> means having —

○ no color at all

○ few colors or dull colors

⬤ many colors or bright colors

○ colors that fade away

TEKS 3.4A

Tip
Identify the suffix and the base word. How does adding the suffix change the meaning of the base word?

2 Which of these best describes the relationship between Clara and Andrew?

⬤ They are good friends and love each other.

○ They do not like each other very much.

○ They like to play tricks on each other.

○ They do not know each other very well.

TEKS 3.8B

3 Why is it important to the plot that Clara has to wait until sundown to see the bats?

⬤ So that Clara figures out the bats will not harm her if it is dark

○ To show Clara getting more nervous as the day goes on

○ So that Clara is able to forget about the bats completely

○ To show that the longer Clara waits, the more excited she gets

TEKS RC-3(D)

Tip
Think about why the author has made the main character wait so long to face her fear. What effect does this have on the plot?

GO ON

Grade 3: Fiction

4 Use the diagram to answer the question.

Clara visits her brother
Andrew in Austin.

↓

She is afraid when she finds
out they will see the Congress
Street Bridge bats.

↓

Andrew sees she is afraid as
they walk toward the park to
watch the bats.

↓

[ ]

Which sentence belongs in the box?

 Clara tries not to think about the bats as she munches on a sandwich.

 To hide her worry, Clara explains, "I don't really love bats."

 Clara gulps when Dad says, "Aww, a few bats won't hurt you."

 Clara is relieved when Andrew suggests they watch the bats from far away.

TEKS 3.8A

Tip
This question is about the order of events. Look back at the story to see when each event happened.

5 Which sentence best states the theme?

A kind act from a loved one can mean a lot.

Fear can make someone do strange things.

Parents always know what is best for their children.

People should always try to overcome their fears.

TEKS 3.5A

6 Which is the best summary of this selection?

Clara is excited to visit her brother Andrew. He plans to take her to see the bats. Clara really fears bats and does not want to go. Her father tells her that it is an amazing sight.

Clara was afraid of bats. Clara came to visit Andrew. Clara finds the bats amazing, but she still says she doesn't like them. She is always happy to see her brother, though.

Clara hoped her brother Andrew would forget about taking her to see the bats. He tells her not to worry. Afterwards, Clara and Andrew hug.

Clara and her family go to visit her brother. Clara is afraid of bats so Andrew suggests watching the bats from far away. Clara is relieved and is able to enjoy the bats without fear.

TEKS RC-3(E)

Grade 3: Fiction

Literary Nonfiction

Genre Overview

Literary nonfiction tells about people who really lived and events that really happened. Authors often use photographs and captions to help readers learn more about the people and events in a story.

An **autobiography** is the story of a person's life written by that person. In an autobiography, the author describes the most important events in his or her life and includes interesting details that tell more about these events. A **biography** is the story of a person's life written by someone else. The author may also include his or her opinions, with details that support them. Both biographies and autobiographies are usually written in time-order, or the sequence in which events happened.

An autobiography is written using the first-person point of view. The author of an autobiography uses words such as *I, me, we,* and *our*. A biography is written using the third-person point of view. The author of a biography uses words such as *he, she, it,* and *they*.

As you read, you may find words that have different meanings depending on how they are used in a sentence. Words with more than one meaning are called **multiple-meaning words**. Sometimes you can figure out the meaning of a multiple-meaning word by looking at the words around it. These context clues can help you figure out which meaning is used. For example, the word *lap* can mean "the part of the body from the waist to the knees when someone is sitting" or "to fall gently against." Here is a sentence using this multiple-meaning word: *The waves lap at the white sand on the beach and slowly wash away our sand castle.* In this case, the words *slowly* and *wash away* are clues that *lap* means "to fall gently against."

Name _____ Date _____

Literary Nonfiction

Read this selection. Then answer the questions that follow it.
Fill in the circle of the correct answer.

The Jim Thorpe Story

1   You can probably name many athletes alive today. You see them in TV ads, in magazines, and sometimes even in movies. Have you ever heard of the athlete Jim Thorpe? Jim Thorpe lived long ago, but he is still known as one of the greatest athletes of all time.

Early Years

2   Jim Thorpe was born on May 28, 1887. He was born in a small cabin in Oklahoma. Jim's mother was a Native American. He grew up around other Native Americans. His family gave him a special name, Wa-Tho-Huk. This means "Bright Path."

3   When Jim was in college, he played for a great coach named Pop Warner. He did well at baseball, football, and track. He was an important athlete in his school.

> **Tip**
>
> Think about the words *Jim* and *he* in paragraphs 2 and 3. How do these words help you know whether this is a biography or an autobiography?

A Gold Medal Winner

4   In 1912, Jim went to the Olympics. He won two gold medals for running. A newspaper said that he had once been paid to play baseball. This was against the rules, so Jim's medals were taken away. His family tried for many years to get them back. Finally, in 1982, Jim's children got the medals back.

> **Tip**
>
> Stop every few paragraphs to summarize the main events. Which details in paragraph 4 would you include in a summary?

A Great Player

5   In the same year that Jim won his medals, he helped his college football team become national champs. He also scored 25 touchdowns and 198 points in one season! This was a great achievement.

Grade 3: Literary Nonfiction

Name _____ Date _____

TEKS 3.2B, 3.4B, 3.9, 3.16, RC-3(D), RC-3(E)

6   Jim still played baseball, too. He played one game on the border between three states. In that game, he hit home runs into all three states! He hit the first over left field into Oklahoma. He hit his second over right field into Arkansas. He hit his third into center field into Texas.

Later Years

7   Over the years, Jim played both football and baseball for many teams. Then, in 1920, he became the first president of the National Football League. He was named one of the world's best athletes by many groups. He died in 1953. Then in 1963, he was elected to the Football Hall of Fame. This great athlete deserved every honor he received.

Tip

Use the headings to find facts from different times in Jim's life.

Football Hall of Fame Web Page

| Hall of Famers | The Hall/Plan a Visit | Football History | Events | Tickets |

New Members for 2010

How Members Are Chosen for the Hall of Fame

Information on Members Past and Present

VISIT US

What's New   Special Offers   Packages

SEARCH [   ]   GO [   ]

GO ON

Name _____ Date _____

1 Read the web below and use it to answer the question.

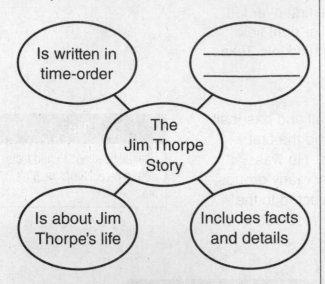

Which of these best completes the web?

- Is about a made-up person

- Is a biography

- Is written by Jim Thorpe about his own life

- Tells how to do something

TEKS 3.9

2 In paragraph 3, which words help the reader know what the word <u>track</u> means?

- *in college*

- *great coach*

- *baseball, football*

- *Pop Warner*

TEKS 3.4B

Tip
Some words have more than one meaning. Figure out the meaning by looking at the words around it.

3 Which sentence from the selection tells what happened to Jim's medals in the end?

- *He won two gold medals for running.*

- *A newspaper said that he had once been paid to play baseball.*

- *His family tried for many years to get them back.*

- *Finally, in 1982, Jim's children got the medals back.*

TEKS 3.2B

Grade 3: Literary Nonfiction

Name _____ Date _____

4 Jim Thorpe is known as one of the greatest athletes of all time because —

○ he played many different sports well

○ the newspapers wrote about him

○ he went to the Olympics in 1912

○ he hit home runs into three states

TEKS RC-3(D)

5 Which is the best summary of paragraphs 4–6?

○ Jim scored 25 touchdowns and 198 points in one football season. He won gold medals in the Olympics, but then they were taken away.

○ In 1912, Jim won two gold medals in the Olympics for running, he helped his college football team become national champs, and he hit home runs playing baseball.

○ Jim's family tried to get the gold medals that were taken from him. In one baseball game, he played on the border between three states.

○ In one baseball game, Jim hit three home runs into Oklahoma, Texas, and Arkansas. He also scored 25 touchdowns in one football season.

TEKS RC-3(E)

> **Tip**
>
> Think about the important events that belong in the summary. Look back at the paragraphs and the events.

6 Refer to the web page. Where would you click to find out more about Jim Thorpe?

○ The Hall/Plan a Visit

○ New Members for 2010

○ Information on Members Past and Present

○ How Members Are Chosen for the Hall of Fame

TEKS 3.16

> **Tip**
>
> Look at the buttons on the top row of the menu. Find the button for people in the Hall of Fame. Which drop-down menu item would have information about a member of the Hall of Fame who was elected in 1963?

Grade 3: Literary Nonfiction

Expository Text

Genre Overview

Expository text gives facts and information about a topic such as baseball, dinosaurs, or worms. As you read expository text, look for the main idea, or central idea, about the topic. The **main idea** tells what the selection is mostly about. Authors of expository text include facts and details that support the main idea and give more information about it.

Authors write expository text for a certain **purpose**, or reason. They might want to give you information about a topic, or they might want to explain how to do something.

An expository text might include causes and effects. A **cause** is the reason that something happens. An **effect** is what happens as a result of the cause. This is an example of a sentence that shows cause and effect: *When the boy kicked the ball, it rolled down the hill*. The cause is "the boy kicked the ball." The effect is "it rolled down the hill."

An expository text may also include directions or steps in a process. This part of the text will be organized by **sequence**. This means the author gives information in a specific order.

Expository text includes **text features** such as bold print, captions, headings, and italics. These features can help you find information. For example, a word in bold print might point out an important idea or the meaning of a word. It might also tell you that a definition or example of the word will follow.

Grade 3: Expository Text

Expository Text

TEKS 3.13A, 3.13C, 3.13D, 3.15B, RC-3(D), RC-3(E)

Expository Text

> **Read this selection. Then answer the questions that follow it.
> Fill in the circle of the correct answer.**

A Worm Bin

1   There are many reasons why you might want to keep a worm bin. People all over the world keep worms to change garbage into **compost,** a rich soil. They feed the worms food scraps. Two pounds of worms can eat a pound of garbage every day. That's a lot of trash.

2   Keeping worms is easy, and it can be a lot of fun. You'll also help our environment by turning trash into compost for houseplants and gardens. The following directions will show you how to make your own worm bin.

> **Tip**
>
> To make something, you need to follow steps in a set of directions. Think of what might happen if you did not follow these steps in order?

How to Make a Worm Bin

Materials

To make a simple worm bin, you will need:

- Plastic container, at least 8 inches deep
- Newspaper
- Soil
- Food scraps
- Water
- Worms

Directions

1. **Prepare the bin.** Ask an adult to poke some small holes through the bottom of the container.

2. **Add the bedding.** Fill half of the container with small pieces of newspaper. Add a cup of soil.

3. **Pour water onto the bedding.** Make sure all of the newspaper is damp, but not soaking wet.

4. **Add the worms.** Slide the worms into the bin.

5. **Feed the worms.** Bury the food scraps in the bedding for the worms to eat.

Grade 3: Expository Text

3   Once you have set up your worm bin, you'll need to maintain it. Keep the bedding moist so it does not dry out. Be sure to feed the worms. Pay attention to how much the worms are eating. Too much food in the bin will start to smell.

4   When the worm bin habitat is starting to work well, you can **harvest**, or gather, the compost. Worms eat their bedding as well as their food. When the bedding is almost gone, push what's left of it to one side and add fresh, damp bedding to the other side. Bury the food scraps in the new bedding. The worms will move to the food. Then you can harvest the compost without taking all the worms with it. Use the compost. It helps plants grow better. Add it to potted plants, or put it in a family or community garden.

> **Tip**
>
> The main idea of a paragraph is often in the first sentence. What is the main idea?

> **Tip**
>
> Use text features such as words in bold print to locate information.

GO ON ➡

Grade 3: Expository Text

Expository Text

TEKS 3.13A, 3.13C, 3.13D,
3.15B, RC-3(D), RC-3(E)

1 In paragraphs 1 and 2, which sentence best supports the main idea that people can have a good time turning trash into compost to help the environment?

○ *That's a lot of trash.*

○ *They feed the worms food scraps.*

○ *Keeping worms is easy, and it can be a lot of fun.*

○ *The following directions will show you how to make your own worm bin.*

TEKS 3.13A

Tip
Read each answer choice. Which one provides the best support for the main idea of the first two paragraphs?

2 The author included the drawings to show—

○ the materials you need to make a worm bin

○ different worm bins from around the world

○ the steps you follow to make a worm bin

○ how worms turn trash into compost

TEKS 3.15B

3 If your worm bin begins to smell, what should you do?

○ Add water

○ Add food

○ Stop adding food for a while

○ Stop adding water for a while

TEKS RC-3(D)

Tip
Reread paragraph 3. What clues can help you figure out the answer?

GO ON

Grade 3: Expository Text

Name _____ Date _____

4 The word **harvest** is in bold print in paragraph 4 to tell you that—

○ it is the most important word in the paragraph

○ a pronunciation of the word follows

○ it is not an English word

○ a meaning of the word follows

TEKS 3.13D

5 Read the chart and use it to answer the question.

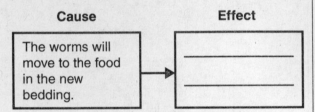

Cause — The worms will move to the food in the new bedding.

Effect — _____

Which sentence belongs on the blank lines?

○ Worms will eat their bedding as well as their food.

○ You can harvest the compost without taking the worms with it.

○ You should bury the food scraps in the new bedding.

○ Compost can help plants grow better in your garden.

TEKS 3.13C

Tip
Ask yourself, "What happens because the worms move to the food in the new bedding?"

6 Which is the best summary of paragraphs 3 and 4?

○ Make sure the bedding in your worm bin does not dry out by adding fresh bedding with food. After the worms move, harvest the compost and add it to plants.

○ Compost helps plants grow better, so add it to potted plants or use it in a garden. Bury the food scraps in the new bedding, and wait for the worms to eat it.

○ Take care of how much food you give your worms. Worms will move to the food if you put food scraps in the new bedding and push the old bedding aside.

○ Too much food in the bin can start to smell bad, so pour water onto the bedding. The worms will eat the food, and the compost you get can be used in many ways.

TEKS RC-3(E)

STOP

© Houghton Mifflin Harcourt Publishing Company

Name _____ Date _____

Drama

Genre Overview

A **drama,** or play, tells a story through words and actions. Like a fiction story, it has characters, setting, and plot. As you read, look for ways that characters change. Look at the way one plot event leads to the next one. Also, look for a theme, or message, that the author gives.

Dramas are divided into sections called **scenes**. The setting usually changes in each scene.

A drama has a **cast of characters**. A character's name, followed by a colon, tells you who is speaking. For example:

TINA: Well, Pablo, did you catch any fish?

The **stage directions** sometimes give information about the setting. For example:

(Time: Sunrise. Setting: A pond near an old wooden farmhouse.)

Stage directions may also describe a character's feelings and actions. For example:

PABLO: *(Proudly)* I caught a big one, but it got away.
TINA: *(With disbelief)* Really? Me, too! *(She puts away her pole.)*

Stage directions are given from the point of view of an actor on the stage. For example, *stage right* means to the actor's right, which is the audience's left.

As you read, you may come across **homographs,** words that are spelled the same but have different meanings. They may be pronounced differently, too. To figure out the correct meaning of these words, look at how they are used in the drama. Think about the meaning of the word *bow* in this sentence: *People bow before the king*. The word *bow* means "to bend the head or body." How is the meaning of *bow* different in this sentence? *She tied a big bow on the box*. In this sentence, the word *bow* means "knot tied with loops." You can use **context clues**, or the words around a homograph, to figure out its meaning in each sentence.

GO ON

Grade 3: Drama

Name _____ Date _____

Drama

Read this selection. Then answer the questions that follow it.
Fill in the circle of the correct answer.

Planting Tulips

Cast of Characters: LUCY MONROE, NITA LOPEZ,
MRS. LOPEZ, MRS. MONROE

Scene: (*Setting: Two houses on a street. LUCY is playing hopscotch on the sidewalk in front of her house. NITA walks out of the house next door with MRS. LOPEZ, her grandmother.*)

1   **NITA:** Hi, Lucy! My grandma is going to teach me how to plant tulips, Want to learn, too?

2   **LUCY:** No thanks. I'm going to watch TV.

(*LUCY runs stage left and inside her house. MRS. MONROE is standing by the door. It is obvious she was listening, and she looks unhappy.*)

3   **MRS. MONROE:** Why don't you want to learn how to plant tulips?

4   **LUCY:** I'd rather watch TV.

5   **MRS. MONROE:** You watch too much TV. That's so nice of Mrs. Lopez to offer to teach you to garden. You should go back over there.

6   **LUCY:** (*Whining*) But Mom …

7   **MRS. MONROE:** Go!

(*LUCY runs through the door and then stage right. She goes around the fence to where NITA and MRS. LOPEZ are kneeling on the ground.*)

8   **LUCY:** (*Pouting*) My mom says I should learn how to garden.

> **Tip**
>
> What do Lucy and Mrs. Monroe argue about that makes Lucy upset? This dialogue introduces the problem in the drama.

Grade 3: Drama

9   **MRS. LOPEZ:** *(Smiling)* I would love to teach you, Lucy! Just grab that trowel and dig a small hole in the dirt. Make sure you dig down about six inches.

(LUCY frowns before grabbing a trowel and kneeling on the ground next to NITA. She digs a hole.)

10   **MRS. LOPEZ:** That looks great! Now drop the bulb in the hole and cover it up with dirt, like this. Next, water the bulb.

(MRS. LOPEZ demonstrates for the girls, and then LUCY and NITA happily follow her lead.)

11   **LUCY:** *(Standing and brushing dirt off of her hands.)* That was really fun! I can't wait to see the garden.

12   **NITA:** When will the flowers bloom?

13   **MRS. LOPEZ:** The tulips won't actually grow until next spring. We plant the bulbs in the fall because they will grow better if they are in the ground all winter.

14   **NITA:** *(Looking sad)* Oh, I thought we'd get to see them right away.

(A clap of thunder sounds. NITA, LUCY, and MRS. LOPEZ are startled and look up.)

15   **NITA:** *(Alarmed)* Grandma! Our tulips!

Tip
Think about what Lucy was like at the beginning of the drama. How has she changed?

Grade 3: Drama

Name _____ Date _____

16   **MRS. LOPEZ:** They'll be okay. The rain will help them grow, and next spring we'll have a beautiful garden!

17   **LUCY:** Thanks for showing me how to plant tulips, Mrs. Lopez. This was way more fun than watching TV.

18   **MRS. LOPEZ:** I'm glad you joined us, Lucy. But remember, our work isn't over. In the spring, we're going to have to take care of the tulips so they grow to be as healthy and pretty as possible.

19   **LUCY:** *(Excited)* I can't wait! Maybe I can pick some as a <u>present</u> for my mom.

(It starts to rain, and they run toward the LOPEZ house.)

(The stage lights go down.)

Tip
Remember the underlined word in paragraph 19. You may be asked a question about it.

1 What event makes Lucy learn how to plant tulips?

⬭ Lucy runs inside her house.

⬭ Lucy grows tired of watching TV.

⬭ Mrs. Monroe learns how to plant tulips herself.

⬭ Mrs. Monroe tells Lucy she must go to the Lopez house.

TEKS 3.8A

Tip

Think back to the beginning of the drama. What happens to make Lucy accept Nita's invitation?

2 What does Nita say that shows she is concerned about the thunder?

⬭ *My grandma is going to teach me how to plant tulips.*

⬭ *Oh, I thought we'd get to see them right away.*

⬭ *Grandma! Our tulips!*

⬭ *When will the flowers bloom?*

TEKS 3.7

Tip

Look back at what Nita says when she hears the thunder and how Mrs. Lopez responds.

3 In paragraph 19, the word <u>present</u> means—

⬭ a gift

⬭ not absent

⬭ at this time

⬭ for a short time

TEKS 3.4B

4 How does Lucy change by the end of the drama?

⬭ She is angry about learning to plant tulips.

⬭ She is happy about learning to plant tulips.

⬭ She no longer wants to be friends with Nita.

⬭ She wants to watch TV most of the time.

TEKS 3.8B

 GO ON

Grade 3: Drama

© Houghton Mifflin Harcourt Publishing Company

5 Read the story map and use it to answer the question below.

Characters	Setting
Lucy, Nita, Mrs. Lopez, Mrs. Monroe	Time: Present Place: Street with two houses

Problem: _____

Solution: Lucy finds that planting tulips is fun.

Which sentence belongs on the blank line?

○ Lucy tries to learn to plant tulips, but she is not good at gardening.

○ Lucy has to learn to plant tulips, but she would rather watch TV.

○ Mrs. Lopez is not a good teacher, so Lucy has a hard time learning.

○ Mrs. Lopez has no time to show her, but Lucy wants to learn to garden.

TEKS 3.7

6 Which sentence best states the theme of this drama?

○ Gardening should only be done by adults.

○ It is important to do whatever makes you happy.

○ If you like something, there is no need to do anything different.

○ You will never know if you like something unless you try it.

TEKS 3.5A

Tip
Think about the main events in the drama. What has Lucy learned by the end?

Grade 3: Drama

Name _____ Date _____

Poetry

Genre Overview

Poetry is a form of writing that tells a story or describes something. It is different from other forms of writing. Poetry uses words in a way that puts a lot of meaning into a small number of words and lines. Other forms of writing are divided into paragraphs, but a poem is often divided into stanzas. A **stanza** is a group of two or more lines in a poem.

Narrative poetry is poetry that tells a story. Like other fiction, a narrative poem has characters, setting, and a plot with a sequence of events. In fiction, the story can be told by a narrator. In narrative poetry, the story is told by a **speaker**.

A poem **rhymes** when two or more lines end with the same sound, such as lines that might end with *pool* and *rule*. A poet may use a pattern of line lengths or **line breaks** to create rhythm in the poem.

A poet might use **sensory language** to help the reader see, hear, or feel something. Sensory language includes similes and metaphors. **Similes** use the words *like* or *as* to compare two things. An example of a simile is *The night sky is as black as ink*. This simile describes a night that is very dark. **Metaphors** compare two things by saying that one thing *is* another thing. An example of a metaphor is *The football player was a tornado on the field*. This metaphor describes a fast and powerful football player. Metaphors do not use the words *like* or *as* to compare.

Sometimes as you read, you will find synonyms. A **synonym** is a word that has the same or nearly the same meaning as another word. See if you can find the synonyms in this sentence: *The large bird spread its big wings and took flight*. The words *large* and *big* are synonyms.

Grade 3: Poetry

Name _____ Date _____

Poetry

> **Read this selection. Then answer the questions that follow it.**
> **Fill in the circle of the correct answer.**

How the Little Kite Learned to Fly

by Katherine Pyle

1   "I never can do it," the little kite said,
    As he looked at the others high over his head.

    "I know I should fall if I tried to fly."
    "Try," said the big kite, "only try!
5   Or I fear you never will learn at all."
6   But the little kite said: "I'm <u>afraid</u> I'll fall."
    The big kite nodded: "Ah, well, good-by;
    I am off." And he rose toward the tranquil sky.

9   Then the little kite's paper stirred at the sight.
10   And trembling he shook himself free for flight.
    First whirling and frightened, then braver grown,
    Up, up he rose through the air alone,
    Till the big kite looking down could see
    The little one rising steadily.

15   Then how the little kite thrilled with pride,
    As he sailed with the big kite side by side!
17   While far below he could see the ground,
18   And the boys like small spots moving round.
    They rested high in the quiet air,
20   And only the birds and clouds were there.

    "Oh, how happy I am," the little kite cried.
    "And all because I was brave and tried."

Tip

This poem tells a story. Stop after each stanza to tell what happened in your own words.

Tip

The poet uses sensory language to help the reader see, hear, or feel something in the poem. What words in line 18 help you see what the boys look like to the little kite?

Grade 3: Poetry

Name _____ Date _____

1 Which word from the poem means about the same as the word <u>afraid</u> in line 6?

- ⬭ *frightened*

- ⬭ *whirling*

- ⬭ *steadily*

- ⬭ *happy*

TEKS 3.4C

Tip
Study each answer choice. Eliminate the ones that do not make sense.

2 In lines 9 and 10, the poet uses the words "stirred at the sight" and "trembling" to —

- ⬭ describe how paper kites behave

- ⬭ tell the reader that the big kite is watching

- ⬭ describe the sound of flying on a windy day

- ⬭ help the reader understand what the little kite is feeling

TEKS 3.10

3 When the big kite sees the little kite rising to join him, the big kite probably feels —

- ⬭ sad

- ⬭ angry

- ⬭ afraid

- ⬭ pleased

TEKS RC-3(D)

Tip
Think about how the big kite acts toward the little kite. Does he want the little kite to learn to fly?

4 In lines 17–18, the poet compares the boys to spots because they —

- ⬭ make trouble

- ⬭ look tiny

- ⬭ are round

- ⬭ are moving

TEKS 3.6

Grade 3: Poetry

© Houghton Mifflin Harcourt Publishing Company

Name _____ Date _____

5 Read the chart and use it to answer the question.

How the Little Kite Learned to Fly

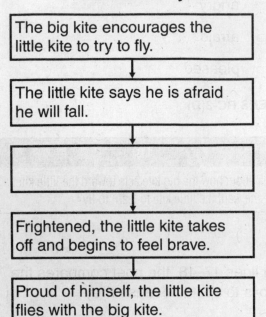

The big kite encourages the little kite to try to fly.

↓

The little kite says he is afraid he will fall.

↓

[empty box]

↓

Frightened, the little kite takes off and begins to feel brave.

↓

Proud of himself, the little kite flies with the big kite.

Which of the following belongs in the empty box?

- ⬭ The big kite takes off and rises toward the sky.
- ⬭ The little kite looks at the others high over his head.
- ⬭ The little kite fills with pride.
- ⬭ The big kite and little kite rest high in the air.

TEKS RC-3(E)

6 Which question is not answered in the poem?

- ⬭ Why does the little kite refuse to fly at first?
- ⬭ What does the little kite see far below him?
- ⬭ How does the little kite feel at the end of the poem?
- ⬭ Who are the boys flying the big kite and the little kite?

TEKS 3.2B

Grade 3: Poetry

Paired Selections

Poetry and Expository Text

Different kinds of texts can talk about the same topic. A **topic** is the subject of the text, or what the text is mostly about. For example, a poem might tell the story of what happened when a family went fishing. An expository text might describe how to fish. The topic of both of these texts is fishing.

After you have read two texts with the same topic, you can **make connections** between them. You might be asked to compare two **genres**, or kinds of texts, such as **poetry** and **expository text**. Sometimes you might compare two genres by looking for similar ideas in both texts. Other times you might contrast them by looking for differences.

Narrative poetry is poetry that tells a story. Like other fiction, a narrative poem has characters, setting, and a plot with a sequence of events. In fiction, the story can be told by a narrator. In narrative poetry, the story is told by a **speaker.**

Sound devices add a musical quality to poetry. A poem **rhymes** when two or more lines end with the same sound. A poet can use a pattern of line lengths, or **line breaks**, to make the poem sound a certain way.

A poet might use words in a special way to help readers picture something. These word pictures are known as **imagery**. One way to create imagery is with sensory language. A poet might use **sensory language** to help the reader see, hear, or feel something.

Expository text gives facts and information about a topic. Expository text states a main idea about the topic and then gives details or facts to support this idea. Sometimes **text features** such as bold print, captions, key words, and italics help you find information.

Authors write expository text for a specific **purpose**, or reason. They might want to give you information about a topic, or they might want to explain how to do something.

Paired Selections

TEKS 3.4C, 3.6, 3.10, 3.12, 3.13B, RC-3(D), RC-3(F)

Paired Selections

> **Read the next two selections. Then answer the questions that follow them.**
> **Fill in the circle of the correct answer.**

Elephant Trouble

1   I looked into my yard one day
    And had to rub my eyes.
    An elephant was standing there,.
    And much to my surprise,

5   He didn't say why he was there.
    I still don't have a clue.
    Perhaps he just got very tired
    Of living in the zoo.

    I knew I had to take him back
10 But how could I do that?
11 Dad's pick-up truck was much too <u>small</u>.
12 Besides, he'd squash it flat!

    That's when I had a brainstorm
    And called my Grandpa Jay.
15 I told him what I needed
    And he brought them right away.

    We laid the small treats on the ground.
    Our big guest ate a few.
    We made a trail right down the street
20 And led him to the zoo.

    So if you find an elephant
    And need to move it quick,
    Just buy a bag of peanuts.
    It's sure to do the trick!

> **Tip**
> Notice that the poem has a story structure. What story parts does the poet describe in stanzas 1 and 2?

> **Tip**
> Think about why the speaker calls the elephant "our big guest." How does the speaker feel about the elephant?

© Houghton Mifflin Harcourt Publishing Company

Grade 3: Paired Selections

Wild Elephants Forever

1   African elephants are huge and powerful animals. They can tear a tree out of the ground with just their long trunks! You might think that such big animals would be safe from anything, but they are not. They are in great danger of disappearing, and there are ways people can help them.

2   African elephants live south of the Sahara Desert in Africa. In 1979, there were about one and a half million elephants. Now, less than one-half million survive. Most live in small patches of forest and grassland and on land set aside by governments.

3   First, people can understand that elephants are often hunted for their valuable tusks. Tusks are the long, pointed bones that stick out of the elephants' mouths. In some countries, it is now against the law to kill elephants or to sell their tusks, but some people still do it.

4   Another way to help is to limit land development. People build roads, houses, and businesses where elephants live. Elephants need a great deal of land to survive. Their grazing lands and homes are shrinking because of the ways that people develop land.

Tip

Paragraph 1 states a main idea: Wild elephants are in danger and people can help them.

Tip

Look for clues to help you draw a conclusion about why these big animals face dangers.

5   Elephants require extremely large areas of grass for both food and for roaming around on. They also drink huge amounts of water every day. So care has to be taken to conserve the land and be sure that there is enough food and water to keep the elephants safe and healthy.

6   The last way people can help wild elephants is to leave them in their natural homes. Sometimes elephants are captured and taken to zoos. Although many zoos treat them well, elephants live best in the wild. Sometimes a captured elephant can escape. Then it becomes a danger to both others and to itself. Only experts in handling elephants should try to rescue it.

7   Wild African elephant herds are getting smaller and smaller. Elephants are gentle animals and they have no natural enemies. The dangers they face are from man and the loss of their natural homes. There are many ways that people can help these huge and powerful animals live longer and better lives.

Tip
Think about the main idea and supporting details that the author provided. Why do you think the author wanted to write this article?

GO ON

Paired Selections

TEKS 3.4C, 3.6, 3.10, 3.12, 3.13B, RC-3(D), RC-3(F)

Use "Elephant Trouble" to answer questions 1 and 2.

---

1 You can tell that "Elephant Trouble" is a narrative poem because it —

- ⬭ uses rhyme
- ⬭ has line breaks
- ⬭ tells a story
- ⬭ gives directions

TEKS 3.6

2 "Besides, he'd squash it flat!" in line 12 appeals mostly to the reader's sense of —

- ⬭ sight
- ⬭ taste
- ⬭ smell
- ⬭ touch

TEKS 3.10

Tip
How does the poet's choice of sensory language help you understand the poem?

Use "Wild Elephants Forever" to answer questions 3 and 4.

---

3 What is the most likely reason the author wrote this article?

- ⬭ To describe what wild elephants look like

- ⬭ To compare different kinds of elephants

- ⬭ To inform the reader about animals in the Sahara Desert

- ⬭ To explain how people can protect wild elephants

TEKS 3.12

4 The author most likely believes that elephants in the circus —

- ⬭ learn important tricks

- ⬭ are lucky to be there

- ⬭ do not belong there

- ⬭ entertain many people

TEKS 3.13B

Tip
Reread paragraph 5. What clues can you find to help you figure out what the author believes?

**Use "Elephant Trouble" and "Wild Elephants Forever" to answer
questions 5 through 8.**

---

5 The word <u>small</u> in the poem is the
opposite of which word from the article?

- ⬭ *huge*
- ⬭ *powerful*
- ⬭ *long*
- ⬭ *safe*

TEKS 3.4C

Tip
Read line 11 of the poem and paragraph 1 of the article to see how the words are used.

6 One idea in both the poem and the
article is —

- ⬭ zoo animals are tame
- ⬭ elephants are very big
- ⬭ people need to help wild elephants
- ⬭ zoos are a good place for elephants

TEKS RC-3(F)

7 Both the speaker of the poem and the
author of the article —

- ⬭ are afraid of elephants
- ⬭ like elephants
- ⬭ think elephants belong in the zoo
- ⬭ have no feelings about elephants

TEKS RC-3(D)

Grade 3: Paired Selections

8 Read the diagram and use it to answer the question.

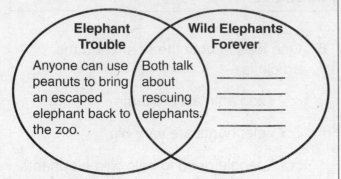

Which of these ideas belongs on the blank lines?

- Any pick-up truck can be used to rescue an escaped elephant.

- Using elephant food is a good way to move an elephant.

- Big cages are the best way to hold an escaped elephant.

- Only experts should try to rescue an escaped elephant.

TEKS RC-3(F)

Tip
The poem and the article have two different ideas about rescuing elephants.

> **Read this selection. Then answer the questions that follow it.**
> **Fill in the circle of the correct answer.**

Mrs. McRitter's Cricket

by Heather A. Meloche

1   Mrs. McRitter collected knickknacks. They covered her tables and bookshelves. They filled her kitchen. They coated her bed and chairs. They even covered Mrs. McRitter, who wore them like jewelry and barrettes in her puffy, curly hair.

2   One day, Mrs. McRitter was getting ready for bed when she heard, "Chirrup!"

3   "Noisy cricket," she said. "But you'll sleep soon." Mrs. McRitter closed her eyes again.

4   "Chirrup!"

5   "Ugh!" Mrs. McRitter shot out of bed. She peered under her bed and behind her chair.

6   She searched around her knickknacks, lifting her tiny glass horses and itty-bitty teacups. She moved the music boxes and rolled around her colored, wooden balls. She shuffled through her crocheted doilies and shook each snow globe.

7   "Where are you?" Mrs. McRitter hollered.

8   "Chirrup!"

9   Mrs. McRitter grabbed a box and threw in her miniature chairs, wooden spoons, and antique spoons. She shoved the box outside and slammed the door.

10   "Chirrup!"

11   "Still not gone!" cried Mrs. McRitter. She snatched up more bags and boxes. All night long she tossed her knickknacks out onto her front lawn. She finished just as the sun rose.

12   Just then, several cars pulled up. People got out and started looking through Mrs. McRitter's knickknacks.

GO ON

13   Mrs. Yan and her daughter Diana approached Mrs. McRitter. "How much for the colored balls?" asked Mrs. Yan.

14   Mrs. McRitter looked surprised, "Oh, they're not for sale. I was just—"

15   "Chirrup!" interrupted the cricket.

16   Mrs. McRitter's head jerked about as she scanned the yard for the cricket.

17   "Well, it's a shame they aren't for sale," said Mrs. Yan, watching Mrs. McRitter stick her face into an open bag.

18   "Chirrup!"

19   "Ugh! I've changed my mind," Mrs. McRitter blurted, raising her frustrated eyes to Mrs. Yan and Diana. "You can have two boxes—no, three—for thirty dollars."

20   Mrs. Yan smiled and handed her the money.

21   "You have a cricket!" said Diana. "You're lucky."

22   "Lucky?" said Mrs. McRitter.

23   "In China, crickets are very lucky," said Diana. We keep them in special cages to hear their beautiful singing."

24   "That's right," said Mrs. Yan. "You should visit us one day and tell us what luck the cricket brings you."

25   "How nice," replied Mrs. McRitter, thinking her cricket brought only trouble.

26   Mrs. Yan and Diana left as Mr. Cornali and his daughter Sara approached Mrs. McRitter.

27   "I love these," said Mr. Cornali, holding a bag of antique spoons.

28   "Chirrup!"

29   "You've got a cricket," Sara said.

30   "Yes," grumbled Mrs. McRitter. "It's horrible."

31 "Not at all!" Sara exclaimed. "Where we come from in Italy, we have a cricket festival. Kids carry their crickets through the streets in special cages. If a cricket sings, the family receives wealth and success that year."

32 Mr. Cornali paid Mrs. McRitter for the spoons. "Visit us sometime and tell us what luck the cricket brings you," he said.

33 "Very kind," muttered Mrs. McRitter, certain the cricket offered more grief than luck.

34 "Chirrup!" sang the cricket from close by.

35 Mrs. McRitter rolled her eyes and dug her hands into her hair.

36 By late morning, Mrs. McRitter had sold all her knickknacks. Certain the cricket was gone, Mrs. McRitter walked into the house and shuffled sleepily down the <u>uncluttered</u> hallway and into her tidy kitchen. She pulled a mug from her organized cupboard and made some tea.

37 In the living room, she nestled into an empty chair and breathed a relaxed sigh.

38 "Chirrup!" said the cricket.

39 "What!" cried Mrs. McRitter, flying up out of her seat. "Impossible!"

40 "Chirrup!"

41 Mrs. McRitter's eyes swept the room and caught her image in a mirror on the wall. She walked closer to the mirror. Then closer. There, nesting in her puffy, curly hair, sat the cricket.

42 "Were you there all along?" cried Mrs. McRitter.

43 "Chirrup!"

44 "But I sold all of my beautiful knickknacks to get rid of you," she moaned, staring at her gloomy, tired face.

45 Then, suddenly, she noticed the reflection of the tidy house around her. On her coffee table sat the money for her knickknacks. The kind faces of the people she had met rose in her mind.

46 "Well, cricket, maybe you aren't that bothersome," admitted Mrs. McRitter.

GO ON

Grade 3: Reading Practice

47 "Chirrup!"

48 "After all, you did bring some wealth."

49 "Chirrup!"

50 "And I made new friends."

51 "Chirrup!"

52 "And my house has never been more comfortable."

53 "Chirrup!" agreed the cricket.

54 "I guess you're good luck after all, cricket," whispered
Mrs. McRitter.

55 "Chirrup!" the cricket sang.

GO ON ➡

Grade 3: Reading Practice

1 How do you know this selection is fiction?

⬭   It is a made-up story written to entertain the reader.

⬭   It explains how to do something.

⬭   It gives facts about a topic.

⬭   It tells events in a real person's life.

TEKS RC-3(D)

2 Which word means about the same as <u>coated</u> in paragraph 1?

⬭   Showed

⬭   Lifted

⬭   Covered

⬭   Cleaned

TEKS 3.4C

3 Who tells this story?

⬭   Mrs. McRitter

⬭   Mrs. Yan

⬭   Mr. Cornali

⬭   A narrator

TEKS 3.8C

4 In paragraph 6, the word <u>knickknacks</u> means —

⬭   large, costly toys

⬭   plain pieces of clothing

⬭   heavy pieces of furniture

⬭   small objects for decoration

TEKS 3.4B

5 What event causes people to visit Mrs. McRitter?

⬭   She tosses her knickknacks out onto her lawn.

⬭   She asks people how to get rid of the cricket.

⬭   She searches for the cricket.

⬭   She catches her image in the mirror on the wall.

TEKS 3.8A

6 In paragraph 19, the reader can tell from Mrs. McRitter's words that she —

⬭   never liked the colored balls.

⬭   wants to get rid of the cricket.

⬭   needs money from Mrs. Yan.

⬭   knows how much Mrs. Yan wants the colored balls.

TEKS RC-3(D)

GO ON

Name _____ Date _____

7 Mrs. McRitter is surprised because her visitors teach her —

○ that having crickets in the house is a problem

○ how much her knickknacks are worth

○ that a cricket brings good luck

○ how to be better organized

TEKS 3.8B

8 Read the chart and use it to answer the question.

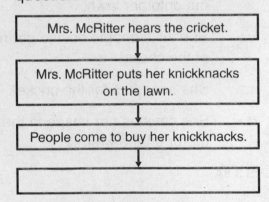

Mrs. McRitter hears the cricket.

↓

Mrs. McRitter puts her knickknacks on the lawn.

↓

People come to buy her knickknacks.

↓

Which sentence belongs in the blank box?

○ Mrs. McRitter gets rid of the cricket.

○ Mrs. McRitter has a tidy house.

○ Mrs. McRitter searches under the bed.

○ Mrs. McRitter gets ready for bed.

TEKS 3.8A

9 What does the word <u>uncluttered</u> mean in paragraph 36?

○ Very messy

○ Messy again

○ Messy with

○ Not messy

TEKS 3.4A

10 How does Mrs. McRitter change by the end of the selection?

○ She is angry that all her things are gone.

○ She is happy to have the cricket.

○ She is upset that the cricket is still there.

○ She is eager to get new things.

TEKS 3.8B

11 Which sentence best states the theme of this selection?

○ You cannot have too many things.

○ Good friends will never let you down.

○ Things happen for the best.

○ Money cannot buy everything.

TEKS 3.5A

46

Grade 3: Reading Practice

**Read this selection. Then answer the questions that follow it.
Fill in the circle of the correct answer.**

Snowflake Bentley

by Jacqueline Briggs Martin

1   In the days when farmers worked with ox and sled and cut the dark with lantern light, there lived a boy who loved snow more than anything else in the world.

2   Willie Bentley's happiest days were snowstorm days. He watched snowflakes fall on his mittens, on the dried grass of Vermont farm fields, on the dark metal handle of the barn door. He said snow was as beautiful as butterflies, or apple blossoms. He could net butterflies and show them to his older brother, Charlie. He could pick apple blossoms and take them to his mother. But he could not share snowflakes because he could not save them.

3   When his mother gave him an old <u>microscope</u>, he used it to look at flowers, raindrops, and blades of grass. Best of all, he used it to look at snow. While other children built forts and pelted snowballs at roosting crows, Willie was catching single snowflakes. Day after stormy day he studied the icy crystals. Their <u>intricate</u> patterns were even more beautiful than he had imagined. He expected to find whole flakes that were the same, that were copies of each other. But he never did. Willie decided he must find a way to save snowflakes so others could see their wonderful designs. For three winters he tried drawing snow crystals. They always melted before he could finish.

4   When he was sixteen, Willie read of a camera with its own microscope. "If I had that camera I could photograph snowflakes," he told his mother. Willie's mother knew he would not be happy until he could share what he had seen.

5   "Fussing with snow is just foolishness," his father said. Still, he loved his son. When Willie was seventeen his parents spent their savings and bought the camera.

Grade 3: Reading Practice

6 It was taller than a newborn calf, and cost as much as his father's herd of ten cows. Willie was sure it was the best of all cameras. Even so his first pictures were failures—no better than shadows. Yet he would not quit. Mistake by mistake, snowflake by snowflake, Willie worked through every storm. Winter ended, the snow melted, and he had no good pictures. He waited for another season of snow. One day, in the second winter, he tried a new experiment. And it worked! Willie had figured out how to photograph snowflakes! "Now everyone can see the great beauty in a tiny crystal," he said.

7 But in those days no one cared. Neighbors laughed at the idea of photographing snow. "Snow in Vermont is as common as dirt," they said. "We don't need pictures." Willie said the photographs would be his gift to the world.

8 While other farmers sat by the fire or rode to town with horse and sleigh, Willie studied snowstorms. He stood at the shed door and held out a black tray to catch the flakes. When he found only jumbled, broken crystals, he brushed the tray clean with a turkey feather and held it out again. He waited hours for just the right crystal and didn't notice the cold. If the shed were warm the snow would melt. If he breathed on the black tray the snow would melt. If he twitched a muscle as he held the snow crystal on the long wooden pick the snowflake would break. He had to work fast or the snowflake would <u>evaporate</u> before he could slide it into place and take its picture. Some winters he was able to make only a few dozen good pictures. Some winters he made hundreds.

9 He wrote about snow and published his pictures in magazines. He gave speeches about snow to faraway scholars and neighborhood skywatchers.

Grade 3: Reading Practice

10   The little farmer came to be known as the world's expert on snow,
"the Snowflake Man." But he never grew rich. He spent every penny
on his pictures. Willie said there were treasures in snow. "I can't afford
to miss a single snowstorm," he told a friend. "I never know when I will
find some wonderful prize." Other scientists raised money so Willie
could gather his best photographs in a book. When he was sixty-six
years old Willie's book—his gift to the world—was published. Even
today, those who want to learn about snow crystals begin with Wilson
Bentley's book, *Snow Crystals*.

GO ON

Grade 3: Reading Practice

1 What tells you this selection is a biography?

- ⬭ It is a made-up story.

- ⬭ It describes a way of doing something.

- ⬭ Wilson Bentley wrote it about his own life.

- ⬭ One person wrote it about another person's life.

TEKS 3.9

2 Read the sentence below from paragraph 2.

> *He watched snowflakes fall on his mittens, on the dried grass of Vermont farm fields, on the dark metal handle of the barn door.*

The author included words like "dried grass of Vermont farm fields" and "dark metal handle" to—

- ⬭ describe Willie's feelings as he watched the snowflakes fall

- ⬭ help the reader understand what Willie was looking at

- ⬭ describe the sound of falling snow on a winter day

- ⬭ tell the reader what falling snowflakes felt like

TEKS 3.10

3 Which dictionary guide words would help you find <u>microscope</u> from paragraph 3?

- ⬭ *mice* and *midday*

- ⬭ *mile* and *mind*

- ⬭ *metal* and *meter*

- ⬭ *melt* and *mend*

TEKS 3.4E

4 In paragraph 3, <u>intricate</u> means —

- ⬭ ugly

- ⬭ simple

- ⬭ ordinary

- ⬭ complicated

TEKS 3.4C

5 Read the chart and answer the question.

Question	Answer	Supporting Detail
What did Willie's parents think of his ideas?	They wanted to help him carry out his dreams.	

Which sentence belongs in the chart?

- ⬭ They bought a special camera.

- ⬭ They said be a photographer.

- ⬭ They got a new microscope.

- ⬭ They told him he was foolish.

TEKS 3.2B

GO ON ➤

Grade 3: Reading Practice

6 From the information in the selection, the reader can tell that Willie —

⬭ got along with his neighbors

⬭ did not give up easily

⬭ loved being a farmer

⬭ had little patience

TEKS RC-3(D)

7 In paragraph 8, why didn't the cold bother Willie as he waited for the right crystal?

⬭ He was wearing layers of clothing to keep warm.

⬭ He was focused on the crystals and not the cold.

⬭ He was numb from the cold, so he couldn't feel it.

⬭ He was used to the cold and it didn't affect him.

TEKS RC-3(D)

8 In paragraph 8, the word <u>evaporate</u> means —

⬭ hard to lift

⬭ not heavy

⬭ dry up

⬭ get wet

TEKS 3.4B

9 Which question is not answered in the selection?

⬭ During what years do these events take place?

⬭ Why wasn't Willie able to draw snow crystals?

⬭ How did Willie get the money to publish his book of photos?

⬭ How old was Willie when he read about a special camera?

TEKS 3.2B

10 Which of these is the best summary of the selection?

⬭ Willie was a farmer, but he was more interested in snow. He stood at the door with a black tray to try to get snowflakes and take pictures of them.

⬭ Willie's mother gave him an old microscope. He wrote about snow and gave speeches to faraway scholars.

⬭ Willie loved snowflakes and wanted to share them with others. He figured out how to photograph snow crystals. He became an expert on snow.

⬭ Willie's neighbors laughed at him for taking photographs of snowflakes. He never wanted to miss a snowstorm.

TEKS RC-3(E)

Name _____ Date _____

Reading
PRACTICE

TEKS 3.4A, 3.4C, 3.12, 3.13A,
3.13B, 3.13C, 3.13D, 3.15B,
RC-3(D), RC-3(E)

**Read this selection. Then answer the questions that follow it.
Fill in the circle of the correct answer.**

Wind

by Nate LeBoutillier

1   Wind blows and swirls. It whistles and moans. Wind pushes sailboats and turns windmills. Wind lifts up kites. When it is hot outside, wind can cool people down. Strong wind can also damage things on Earth and even harm people.

What Is Wind?

2   The sun causes wind. The imaginary line around the middle part of Earth is called the equator. The sun's light hits Earth most directly at the equator and makes it hot. The North Pole and South Pole get less direct light from the sun. They are very cold.

3   Heating makes air <u>expand</u>. Air that is less dense rises. Cooling makes air contract. Denser air sinks. When hot air mixes with cold air, the cooler air scoots under the warmer air. This makes wind.

Harmful Wind

4   Sometimes wind can be very strong. When wind gets wild, storms happen. Hurricanes or cyclones are windstorms that start out in the ocean. They spin water and waves onto land.

5   Tornadoes are windstorms that come down from clouds. They can be very scary and <u>powerful</u>. Some tornadoes pick up trees and houses or even animals and people!

Grade 3: Reading Practice

Name _____ Date _____

Reading
PRACTICE

TEKS 3.4A, 3.4C, 3.12, 3.13A,
3.13B, 3.13C, 3.13D, 3.15B,
RC-3(D), RC-3(E)

6   Blizzards are windstorms that blow snow and cold air so hard that it can be hard to see! Every year, some people around the world get hurt or even killed by windstorms.

Helpful Wind

7   Wind can help people in many ways, too. Wind that blows through windmills creates electricity. Electricity is a useful form of energy. Many things in houses use energy, such as TVs, washing machines, and hair dryers.

8   Wind can be used to help people travel, too. Wind can push sailboats and ships. Wind helps airplanes fly faster and farther. Some people are building cars that use wind to make themselves go! Wind that makes a bad storm can also push the storm away.

9   Whether wind is helping people or causing problems, one thing is for sure. All around the world, the wind is always blowing!

TEKS 3.4A, 3.4C, 3.12, 3.13A,
3.13B, 3.13C, 3.13D, 3.15B,
RC-3(D), RC-3(E)

Hands-On: Wind Spinner

Make a spinner to watch the power of the wind!

What You Need

- a pushpin
- scissors
- a sharpened pencil with eraser
- a square piece of construction paper

What You Do

1. Draw lines from corner to corner to form a large "X" on your paper. Punch a small hole with the pencil tip at the point where the lines cross.

2. Cut along each line, stopping about an inch (2.5 cm) from the hole.

3. Make a pin hole in the top left corner of each flap. Fold each punched corner toward the center hole.

4. Line up the holes. Push the pin through them and into the side of the eraser at the end of the pencil.

Hold your spinner facing the wind and watch it go!

1 Read the sentence below from paragraph 1.

> *When it is hot outside, wind can cool people down.*

Under which heading might you find information that explains this idea?

- ○ **What Is Wind?**
- ○ **Harmful Wind**
- ○ **Helpful Wind**
- ○ **Hands-On: Wind Spinner**

TEKS 3.13D

2 From the information in the selection, the reader can tell that—

- ○ places at the equator are drier
- ○ places near the equator are wetter
- ○ places far from the equator are hotter
- ○ places far from the equator are colder

TEKS 3.13B

3 Which word means the opposite of expand in paragraph 3?

- ○ *dense*
- ○ *contract*
- ○ *mixes*
- ○ *under*

TEKS 3.4C

4 Wind is caused by —

- ○ cooler air moving under warmer air
- ○ water that spins and washes onto land
- ○ the sun's light hitting Earth directly
- ○ cooling air that expands

TEKS 3.13C

5 What does the word powerful mean in paragraph 5?

- ○ full of strength
- ○ without strength
- ○ one who has strength
- ○ one who is the strongest

TEKS 3.4A

GO ON

55

Grade 3: Reading Practice

Name _____ Date _____

Reading
PRACTICE

TEKS 3.4A, 3.4C, 3.12,
3.13A, 3.13B, 3.13C, 3.13D,
3.15B, RC-3(D), RC-3(E)

6 Use the main ideas and details below to answer the question.

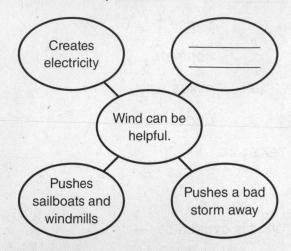

Which detail best completes the web?

○ Blows snow and cold air

○ Helps airplanes fly faster

○ Spins waves onto land

○ Picks up trees and houses

TEKS 3.13A

7 What is the most likely reason the author wrote "Wind"?

○ To explain how people can stay safe in storms

○ To entertain people with interesting stories

○ To describe the weather in different places

○ To give facts about wind

TEKS 3.12

8 Which is the best summary of this selection?

○ Wind helps people or causes them problems.

○ The sun causes wind by giving direct and indirect light.

○ Wind can harm people and cause powerful storms.

○ Wind can help people make electricity and travel.

TEKS RC-3(E)

9 Which of the following is not something you need to make a wind spinner?

○ Construction paper

○ A pushpin

○ Scissors

○ A hole puncher

TEKS 3.15B

10 According to the wind spinner directions, what do you hold when you point the wind spinner into the wind?

○ End of the pin

○ Bottom of the pencil

○ Handle of the scissors

○ Construction paper flaps

TEKS RC-3(D)

Grade 3: Reading Practice

> **Read this selection. Then answer the questions that follow it.**
> **Fill in the circle of the correct answer.**

Pecos Bill and the Stampede

Cast of Characters: NARRATOR, MAN 1, WOMAN, MAN 2,
TELEGRAPH OPERATOR, PECOS BILL, JACK, HANK

Scene 1 (*Setting: A small Texas town in the 1840s. A group of townspeople have gathered outside the general store. The NARRATOR is stage left, facing the audience.*)

1 **NARRATOR:** Pecos Bill had a strange childhood. While his family was moving west, he fell out of the back of the wagon into the Pecos River. His parents didn't know he was missing until it was too late. So, Bill was <u>raised</u> by coyotes. His brother found him one day and taught him how to be a cowboy. And Bill became the best cowboy in the world! He came to own a big ranch. How big? Some say he used New Mexico as a corral and Arizona as a pasture. Things were going fine until one horrible day. Let's listen to find out what's happening. (*Turns toward the townspeople.*)

2 **MAN 1:** (*Excitedly*) What's that loud roar?

3 **WOMAN:** (*Points toward cloud of dust*) And look at that giant cloud of dust rising in the east! It must be a stampede!

4 **MAN 2:** (*Alarmed*) Why, Pecos Bill's longhorns are on the run! That herd is racing toward Odessa. The cattle will smash everything in their path. We have to warn those folks!

(*The telegraph operator enters stage left and runs up to the group.*)

5 **TELEGRAPH OPERATOR:** The herd has knocked down the telegraph poles. There's no way to send a warning to Odessa. Hundreds of folks are in danger!

(*The stage lights go down.*)

Name _____ Date _____

Scene 2 *(Setting: The Texas prairie, a few miles in front of the herd. PECOS BILL and JACK, a young cowboy, are resting in the shade of a tall cactus. Their horses are nearby. BILL's horse, Lightning, is bigger and tougher than the other horse.)*

(A loud rumble is heard. BILL jumps up.)

6   **PECOS BILL:** *(Points skyward.)* Jack, look at that dust cloud rising into the sky. Our herd must be stampeding.

7   **JACK:** I'm afraid for those folks in Odessa. The herd will flatten that poor town!

8   **PECOS BILL:** *(Annoyed)* Fear isn't going to help them. Come with me to stop the herd.

9   **JACK:** Not me! When 5,000 head of cattle get loose, you've got Texas-sized trouble. I'm not going near that herd!

10   **PECOS BILL:** *(Shakes his head.)* You disappoint me, son. Go tell the others what's happening. I'll stop that herd by myself. *(Faces his horse.)* Come on, Lightning. We have work to do.

(BILL hurries off stage right, leading Lightning. JACK and his horse leave stage left. The stage lights go down.)

Scene 3 *(Setting: The Texas prairie. JACK and HANK, another of BILL's cowhands, stand on a hill. They are facing in the direction of the stampede. The audience can't see what they see. The NARRATOR is stage left, facing the audience.)*

11   **NARRATOR:** Pecos Bill was <u>fearless</u>, so he didn't wait for help. Lightning ran at lightning speed, and the herd was soon in sight. Jack and Hank will tell you what's going on. *(Faces JACK and HANK.)*

12   **JACK:** Look! Pecos Bill and Lightning are dashing down into the valley after the cattle. Bill is reaching for his rope.

13   **HANK:** He's formed a lasso. Why, he's twirling it faster and faster! It's as big around as a pasture! He's throwing it at the herd.

14   **JACK:** It just snagged the lead animals and dropped around the rest of the herd. Now Bill is pulling the rope tight and yanking the reins to stop Lightning.

Reading
PRACTICE

TEKS 3.2B, 3.4A, 3.4B, 3.5A,
3.7, 3.8A, 3.8B, RC-3(D),
RC-3(E)

15   **HANK:** Oh, no! The horse can't stop! She's dug in her hooves, but the herd just keeps running toward Odessa. They're not far from Main Street now. How will Bill ever stop them?

16   **JACK:** Wait! Bill has an even longer rope. He's making another lasso with his free hand. He's throwing it on a high hill over the valley. That'll act like a brake to stop the herd. *(Pulls back with his hand and arm in a braking motion.)*

17   **HANK:** But can he hold on? He's struggling. No, he's holding on tight. And that hill isn't moving. But if that herd doesn't stop soon, Bill will have to let go of one rope or the other!

18   **JACK:** *(Hides his eyes with his hands.)* I can't look.

19   **HANK:** *(Pulls JACK's hands down.)* Look! They've stopped! Bill has done it! Hurray!

20   **JACK:** From now on, I'm going to be more like Bill. Fear won't get the best of me again.

21   **NARRATOR:** *(Faces the audience.)* Once again, Pecos Bill has saved the day. Didn't I tell you he's the best cowboy in the world?

(The stage lights go down.)

Name _____ Date _____

1 How do you know that this selection is a drama?

- ⬭ It has stage directions.
- ⬭ It has a cast of characters.
- ⬭ It is told through the words and actions of characters.
- ⬭ All of the above

TEKS RC-3(D)

2 What does the word raised mean in paragraph 1?

- ⬭ Gathered together
- ⬭ Lifted higher
- ⬭ Cared for
- ⬭ Stirred up

TEKS 3.4B

3 Which event comes before Pecos Bill sees the dust cloud rising into the sky?

- ⬭ Pecos Bill asks Jack to come with him to stop the herd.
- ⬭ The telegraph operator says the poles are down.
- ⬭ Pecos Bill throws a lasso around the herd.
- ⬭ Pecos Bill throws a lasso around a hill.

TEKS 3.8A

4 From paragraphs 8–10, the reader can tell that —

- ⬭ Pecos Bill feels like Jack has let him down
- ⬭ Jack does not like Pecos Bill
- ⬭ Pecos Bill understands why Jack is afraid
- ⬭ Jack is embarrassed by Bill

TEKS 3.8B

5 What does the word fearless mean in paragraph 11?

- ⬭ Full of fear
- ⬭ Without fear
- ⬭ Easily scared
- ⬭ Becoming afraid

TEKS 3.4A

6 What event resolves the problem?

- ⬭ Pecos Bill leads the herd into a pasture away from town.
- ⬭ Pecos Bill rides in front of the herd and stares them down.
- ⬭ Pecos Bill throws ropes around the herd and over a hill.
- ⬭ Pecos Bill ropes the lead animals and the others fall.

TEKS 3.7

GO ON ➡

60

Grade 3: Reading Practice

Name _____ Date _____

Reading
PRACTICE

TEKS 3.2B, 3.4A, 3.4B,
3.5A, 3.7, 3.8A, 3.8B,
RC-3(D), RC-3(E)

7 Use the chart to answer the question.

Jack at the beginning	Jack at the end
Afraid to help	

Which of these belongs in the blank box?

- ○ Angry at Bill for going alone
- ○ Praises Bill on his skills
- ○ Upset that Bill needs his help
- ○ Decides to be brave, like Bill

TEKS 3.8B

8 The next time Bill asks, Jack will likely —

- ○ help him right away
- ○ refuse to help his friend
- ○ think it over before answering
- ○ ask someone else to help Bill

TEKS RC-3(D)

9 Which is the theme of this selection?

- ○ Think carefully before you act.
- ○ Face challenges bravely.
- ○ Never scold others.
- ○ Heroes do not expect praise.

TEKS 3.5A

10 Which of these is the best summary of the selection?

- ○ Townspeople are afraid that a stampede is headed for Odessa. Pecos Bill sees the herd but cannot get anyone to help him. He takes off on Lightning to stop the herd.

- ○ Pecos Bill is the best cowboy in the world. He was raised by coyotes. He sees that a herd from his ranch has started to stampede, so he stops them.

- ○ A herd is stampeding and hundreds of people are in danger. The townspeople are worried. Jack and Hank watch Pecos Bill try to stop the herd.

- ○ A stampede is headed for Odessa. Pecos Bill takes off on Lightning to stop the herd. Bill throws a lasso over a hill and stops them and saves Odessa.

TEKS RC-3(E)

11 In which book would you most likely find more information about Pecos Bill?

- ○ *Stampede: Old West Dangers*
- ○ *Biographies of Texas Heroes*
- ○ *Famous Texas Folktales*
- ○ *Great Texas Ranchers*

TEKS 3.2B

Grade 3: Reading Practice

**Read this selection. Then answer the questions that follow it.
Fill in the circle of the correct answer.**

Listen, Rabbit!

by Aileen Fisher

1   I saw him first
    when the sun went down
    in the summer sky
    at the edge of town
5   where grass grew green
    and the path grew brown.

    I couldn't tell
    what he was at all
    when I saw him first,
10 sort of halfway small,
    sort of halfway grown,
    near a gray old stone
    in the field, alone.

    Then I saw his ears
15 standing rabbit tall!

Grade 3: Reading Practice

16 I stood as still
      as a maple tree
      and I looked at him
      and he looked at me . . .
20 with only one eye
      that I could see,
22 <u>bulging</u> out
      on the side of his head.

      "Nice little rabbit,"
25 I softly said
      inside myself,
      though I hoped he'd hear
      with two long ears
      standing up so near
30 and my thoughts so <u>clear</u>.

      My heart went thump!
      And do you know why?
      'Cause I hoped that maybe
      as time went by
35 the rabbit and I
      (if he felt like *me*)
      could have each other
      for company.

GO ON

63

1 Read the diagram below and use it to answer the question.

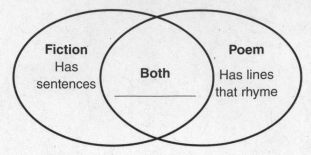

Which of these belongs on the blank line?

- ⬭ Tell a real person's life story
- ⬭ Explain how to do something
- ⬭ Tell a story
- ⬭ Include stage directions

TEKS 3.6

2 What setting does the poet describe when she first sees the rabbit?

- ⬭ A summer evening in a field
- ⬭ Tall green grass near a maple tree
- ⬭ A gray stone wall
- ⬭ Beside the road in the spring

TEKS 3.6

3 Which words does the poet use to describe what the rabbit looks like?

- ⬭ *sort of halfway small, / sort of halfway grown,*
- ⬭ *at the edge of town / where grass grew green*
- ⬭ *"Nice little rabbit," / I softly said*
- ⬭ *and I looked at him / and he looked at me . . .*

TEKS 3.10

4 In lines 16–17, the poet compares herself to a maple tree because both she and a tree —

- ⬭ provide shade
- ⬭ are very tall
- ⬭ have many branches
- ⬭ do not move

TEKS 3.6

5 Why does the poet stand still when she sees the rabbit?

- ⬭ She is waiting for more rabbits.
- ⬭ She does not want to scare the rabbit away.
- ⬭ She does not want the rabbit to see her.
- ⬭ She is frightened of the rabbit.

TEKS RC-3(D)

GO ON ➡

Name _____   Date _____

6 In line 22, the word <u>bulging</u> means —

    ⬭ closing tightly

    ⬭ moving inward

    ⬭ turning around

    ⬭ swelling outward

    TEKS 3.4B

7 Which of the following events happens first?

    ⬭ The poet stands very still.

    ⬭ The poet notices the ears on the rabbit.

    ⬭ The poet sees something near an old gray stone.

    ⬭ The poet thinks, "Nice little rabbit."

    TEKS 3.8A

8 Which word means the opposite of <u>clear</u> in line 30?

    ⬭ Messy

    ⬭ Unknown

    ⬭ Truthful

    ⬭ Simple

    TEKS 3.4C

9 Why does the poet's heart go thump when she meets the rabbit?

    ⬭ She wants to catch him.

    ⬭ She wants to make friends with him.

    ⬭ She wants to take a picture of him.

    ⬭ She has always loved rabbits.

    TEKS 3.8A

10 Which is the best summary of this poem?

    ⬭ The poet is walking at the edge of town at sundown. She sees something in the field but cannot make out what it is. Finally, she sees it is a rabbit.

    ⬭ The poet sees a rabbit in the field. They look at each other. The poet thinks that in time she and the rabbit might enjoy each other's company.

    ⬭ The poet's heart goes thump. She sees a rabbit all alone near a gray stone. The rabbit's ears are standing tall.

    ⬭ The poet talks to herself when she sees a rabbit. The rabbit looks at her. The poet stands very still as the rabbit watches her.

    TEKS RC-3(E)

Grade 3: Reading Practice

Name _____ Date _____

Reading
PRACTICE

TEKS 3.4A, 3.4B, 3.9, 3.13A,
3.15A, RC-3(D), RC-3(E),
RC-3(F)

**Read the next two selections. Then answer the questions that follow them.
Fill in the circle of the correct answer.**

John Chapman, the Real Johnny Appleseed

1   In 1774, John Chapman was born on a small farm in Massachusetts. When he was a boy, John's father sent him to work for a neighbor who had apple orchards. John learned a lot about growing apple trees. Settlers passing through John's town told stories of great stretches of open land in the west. John dreamed of moving there to plant trees of his own.

2   When John was eighteen years old, he left home. He traveled from Massachusetts all the way to Pennsylvania. There, he got free apple seeds at cider mills. Why did the mills give out free seeds? They wanted more apples grown so they could make more apple cider.

3   As he traveled, John Chapman planted the apple seeds on land that wasn't owned by anybody. Then he built fences to <u>protect</u> the growing trees. John made sure the young plants had good soil, water, sunshine, and care. In a few years, he sold the trees to farmers and people arriving from the east. These settlers paid him with cash, food or other things to trade. He often spent time with the settlers, sharing meals and telling stories.

4   John stayed a few years in Pennsylvania planting apple trees. Then he went further west into Ohio, Indiana, and Michigan, where there was even more open land. He kept moving from place to place, but always came back east to get more apple seeds and to check on his trees. He did this for many years.

5   People started telling stories about John. They called him Johnny Appleseed because he planted so many apple seeds. Some people thought he just scattered seeds everywhere he walked, but really it took planning and hard work. He planted seeds only in places that were good to grow apple trees. Even with this hard work, John always found time to help others in need.

Name _____ Date _____

Reading
PRACTICE

TEKS 3.4A, 3.4B, 3.9, 3.13A,
3.15A, RC-3(D), RC-3(E),
RC-3(F)

6   John wore old clothing, and he kept moving from place to place, even though he had enough money to settle down and buy new clothes and a house. No one knows for certain why he dressed the way he did. This made him different from most farmers. People added to the colorful tales they told about John. These stories were not true, but Johnny Appleseed was becoming a legend!

7   In the winter of 1845, John Chapman was 71 years old. He heard that cows had broken down one of his fences. He walked fifteen miles through the cold to fix it. He finally had to stop working.

8   In the end, John left a gift of thousands of apple trees and more than 800 acres of land to the people of the United States. From Pennsylvania to Indiana, John Chapman's apple trees blossomed in the spring and gave tasty fruit in the fall. The United States was a young country, and the apple trees helped settlers as they moved farther west. This is why we still tell the story of Johnny Appleseed today.

Name _____ Date _____

Reading
PRACTICE

TEKS 3.4A, 3.4B, 3.9, 3.13A,
3.15A, RC-3(D), RC-3(E),
RC-3(F)

Up, Down, and Turned Around

1   Does a seed have a top and a bottom? Can it tell up from down?
Can you make its root reach for the sky and its stem grow down to
the ground?

2   Find out by watching your own bean seeds grow.

You Need
paper towels
clear glass jar
colored paper
bean seeds

1. Soak the beans in water overnight.

2. Line the inside of the jar with colored paper. (You can skip this step, but
it makes it easier to see the beans growing.)

3. Fill the jar with wet, crumpled paper towels.

4. Place the beans between the colored paper and the glass. Leave space
around each bean, and turn them in different directions.

5. Look at your beans every day. Add water when needed to keep the
paper towels wet.

6. After two or three days, you'll see a white root push out of each bean.

7. A few days later, you'll see a green stem start to grow and more roots
growing from the main root. Are the roots all growing in the same
direction? What about the stems?

Grade 3: Reading Practice

Name _____   Date _____

What Happened?

3   It doesn't matter which way you plant the seeds. The roots try to grow down toward the ground, and the stems try to grow up.

4   How do they know which way is which? They feel Earth's gravity. Gravity is the <u>invisible</u> force that keeps you on the ground and pulls things down when you drop them. When it feels gravity's pull, a growing root or stem can tell which way is up and which is down.

Grade 3: Reading Practice

Name _____   Date _____

Reading
PRACTICE

TEKS 3.4A, 3.4B, 3.9,
3.13A, 3.15A, RC-3(D),
RC-3(E), RC-3(F)

**Use "John Chapman, the Real Johnny Appleseed" to answer
questions 1 through 4.**

---

1 You can tell that the selection is a
biography because —

- ⬭ it is told through words and
  actions

- ⬭ it is about a real person

- ⬭ John Chapman wrote it himself

- ⬭ one person wrote it about
  another person's life

TEKS 3.9

2 In paragraph 3, the word <u>protect</u> means —

- ⬭ to keep safe from harm

- ⬭ to stop from harming others

- ⬭ to keep from getting out

- ⬭ to cover carefully

TEKS 3.4B

3 From the information in the selection, the
reader can tell that John Chapman —

- ⬭ did not like living in the east

- ⬭ wanted to settle in one place

- ⬭ felt good will towards others

- ⬭ never got along with his family

TEKS RC-3(D)

4 Read the chart and use it to answer the
question.

Events for a Summary
• As a boy, John Chapman worked for a neighbor and learned a lot about growing apple trees.
• _____ _____
• He planted apple seeds and later sold the trees to settlers.
• He planted more seeds in states farther west and became known as Johnny Appleseed.
• He got sick while trying to care for his apple trees.

Which sentence belongs in the chart?

- ⬭ He was born on a small farm
  in Massachusetts.

- ⬭ He dreamed of moving west to
  plant trees of his own.

- ⬭ He heard that cows had
  broken down one of his fences.

- ⬭ He often shared meals and
  stories with the settlers.

TEKS RC-3(E)

GO ON

Grade 3: Reading Practice

Use "Up, Down, and Turned Around" to answer questions 5 through 8.

5 Look at the steps for growing beans. Explain why it is important to turn the beans in different directions.

○ It helps the roots and stems grow faster.

○ It helps more roots and stems grow.

○ It shows the direction of roots and stems.

○ It makes stems turn green.

TEKS 3.15A

6 What should you do after you turn the beans in different directions?

○ Fill the jar with wet, crumpled paper towels

○ Check the beans and keep the paper towels wet

○ Line the inside of the jar with colored paper

○ Soak the beans in water overnight

TEKS 3.15A

7 Which of the following shows that gravity is working on the bean seeds?

○ A white root pushes out of each bean seed.

○ The roots grow down, and the stems grow up.

○ The bean seeds can be turned in different directions.

○ After a few days, more roots grow from the main root.

TEKS 3.13A

8 What does the word <u>invisible</u> mean in the last paragraph?

○ Often seen

○ Seen again

○ Seen with

○ Not seen

TEKS 3.4A

71

Grade 3: Reading Practice

Name _____ Date _____

Reading
PRACTICE

TEKS 3.4A, 3.4B, 3.9,
3.13A, 3.15A, RC-3(D),
RC-3(E), RC-3(F)

Use "John Chapman, the Real Johnny Appleseed" and "Up, Down, and Turned Around" to answer questions 9 through 12.

---

9 Based on both of these selections, you can tell that —

○ seeds need care to grow into plants

○ people can get rich from planting seeds

○ John Chapman planted his seeds upside down

○ gravity is not important for growing apple seeds

TEKS RC-3(F)

10 Based on these selections, which of the following do both bean and apple seeds need to grow?

○ Soil

○ Water

○ Plant food

○ Strong sunlight

TEKS RC-3(F)

11 From information in both selections, the reader can tell that whenever John Chapman planted his seeds —

○ the rich soil in the west helped them grow

○ all the seeds he planted turned into healthy trees

○ gravity helped the roots and stems know how to grow

○ the seeds that got the least water grew the best

TEKS RC-3(F)

12 Both selections show that people who grow things need to—

○ plant seeds first as an experiment

○ cover the seeds with a lot of soil

○ plant the seeds in the ground

○ check on the growing plants

TEKS RC-3(F)

Grade 3: Reading Practice

Name _____ Date _____

Writing a One-Page Composition

Responding to a Prompt

Do you write in a journal? Do you use email? Do you write reports for school? You probably know that people use writing every day. It is important to know how to write well. Writing well means:

- Writing about one personal experience or central idea
- Organizing your ideas in a way that makes sense
- Adding details and examples to make your ideas clear

On a test, you will be given a writing prompt. The prompt will ask you to write a one-page personal narrative or a one-page expository composition. The prompt will include rules to follow when you write. These rules are **READ** or **LOOK, THINK,** and **WRITE**. Read the prompt carefully to make sure you understand it.

Step 1: Plan Your Composition

It is important to organize your ideas before you start writing. Think about these examples:

- A prompt asks you to write a personal narrative about an important event in your life. On a separate sheet of paper, you can draw a web such as the one on the right. Write the important event in the center circle. Then list details about the event in the other circles. Decide which details to keep, and cross out the rest. Now, you are ready to write a first draft. Your composition can be no longer than one page.

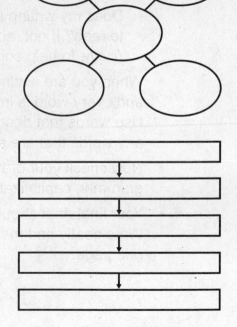

- Another prompt asks you to write an expository composition explaining how to do something. You can use a flowchart like the one on the right. At the top of the flowchart, write a topic sentence that tells your **central idea.** Then list each step or detail in your explanation in the boxes. Make sure your steps are in logical order and support your central idea. Now, you are ready to write a first draft of your expository composition.

Grade 3: Writing Lesson

Step 2: Draft Your Composition

Use the ideas in your graphic organizer to write a first draft. Your composition should have a clear beginning, middle, and ending. Use details and examples to support your ideas.

Step 3: Revise and Edit Your Composition

Reread your draft. Make sure you have correctly answered the writing prompt. Then, look for ways to make your writing better. For example:

- As you reread your personal narrative, look for sentences that are not about the event you are describing. Delete those sentences or add new sentences.

- As you reread your expository composition, delete or rewrite sentences that do not support the central idea. Make sure you have a strong concluding statement.

- For each type of composition, ask yourself questions like these:

  - Does every sentence have a clear purpose? If not, delete or rewrite it.

  - Is every sentence in the best place? If not, move it.

  - Does my writing seem choppy? Change the lengths of some of the sentences.

  - Does my writing flow smoothly? Is it easy for another person to read? If not, add transition words, such as *next, then,* and *finally,* to help connect the ideas.

- When you are writing a one-page composition, every sentence and every word is important. Look again at your word choices. Use words that describe something in an interesting way. Delete any words that are not necessary.

- Now check your draft for errors. Correct errors in spelling, grammar, capitalization, and punctuation.

- Your final draft should include all of the changes you made. Write neatly and make sure your composition is no longer than one page.

Grade 3: Writing Lesson

Name _____ Date _____

Written Composition:
Personal Narrative

LOOK

Look at the picture in the box below.

THINK

Sometimes a person can give you good advice.

Think about good advice you have gotten from a friend or family member. Then think about how you used that person's advice.

WRITE

Write a one-page personal narrative about a time when you took good advice from someone.

As you write your composition, remember to —

❏ describe a time you took someone's good advice.

❏ organize ideas in order. Use transition words.

❏ develop your ideas with details about feelings.

❏ use correct spelling, punctuation, grammar.

❏ make sure your composition is just one page.

Grade 3: Personal Narrative

Sample Response: Personal Narrative

> Write a one-page personal narrative about a time when you took good advice from someone.

The writer shares his thoughts and feelings.

I used to think there was nothing to learn about catching a fish. Then my grandpa took me fishing. Let me tell you about our fishing trip.

Last summer my grandpa gave me a fishing rod. He likes to fish a lot, so I thought it would be fun to try it. Off we went to the pond. I usually like to try something myself before I ask how to do it. So right away, I baited the hook and dropped it into the water.

The writer uses time-order words to connect ideas.

After awhile I was getting hot in the sun. I hadn't caught anything. I started to think that fishing was no fun at all. Then Grandpa came over and showed me how fishermen throw the line. I learned how to flick the rod so the bait would land way out in the pond. I practiced what he showed me. Before I knew what was happening, I had a fish on my line!

Name _____ Date _____

Sample Response: Personal Narrative

> Write a one-page personal narrative about a time when you took good advice from someone.

The writer does not organize ideas in a logical order.

I wanted to play on a basketball team at the YMCA after school. I sent in my forms. My problem was I just sat and waited to hear from them. Everybody kept asking when do the games start? I practiced every day at Tommy's house. He said he didn't kno when the tryouts are. My grandpa wanted to come watch. He always likes to see me play. I said none of my friends had heard anything about when though.

Grandpa told me I better call the YMCA and find out something. Sometimes something's happening and you don't know it is. I didn't think he was right, but you don't say no to grandpa. The YMCA said they made mistakes on the paperwork. They said if I came down right after school the next day I could get in the tryouts. That was lucky for me that I listen to Grandpa.

The writer uses an incorrect verb tense for "listen," which could confuse readers.

Written Composition: Personal Narrative

READ

Read the story in the box below.

> Steve was afraid of swimming. When his mother suggested lessons, Steve decided to face his fear. The teacher started the lessons slowly. Steve discovered that swimming was not as scary as he had thought. By the time the lessons were over, Steve knew how to swim. Something he feared had turned out just fine.

THINK

Think of a time you were afraid of something. Then think about how you got over your fear.

WRITE

Write a one-page personal narrative about a time when you were afraid of something that turned out fine.

As you write your composition, remember to —

❏ describe a personal experience—a time something you feared turned out fine.

❏ organize your ideas, and connect them using transitions.

❏ develop your ideas with details that will help the reader understand your experience and your feelings.

❏ use correct spelling, capitalization, punctuation, grammar, and sentences.

❏ make sure your composition is not longer than one page.

Tip
Before you begin writing, brainstorm vivid words that describe how you felt as you faced your fear.

Tip
Make sure your narrative has a strong beginning and a concluding sentence that tells how events worked out.

Name _____ Date _____

Sample Response: Personal Response

> Write a one-page personal narrative about a time when you were afraid of something that turned out fine.

The writer includes important events and details.

The writer uses his own voice to let the reader know how he feels.

Have you ever been afraid of something but you didn't want anyone to know? I have. I'm afraid of snakes. One day last week I had to do something about it.

The problem started when a ranger from the Wildlife Zoo visited our classroom. He talked about animals from the zoo. Then he reached into a big bag and pulled out a long, thick, black snake. My stomach turned to jelly.

The ranger told volunteers they could come up and handle the snake. My stomach started to hurt. Billy picked up the snake first. Then he held it out to me. My stomach flip-flopped, but I didn't want Billy to know I was afraid. So I took the snake. It felt cold and slippery and strong. I counted to ten while I held that snake up with both hands. Then I passed it to Fern.

All of a sudden I saw it — I had held a snake in my hands! I felt like I could do anything.

Grade 3: Personal Narrative

Sample Response: Personal Narrative

> Write a one-page personal narrative about a time when you were afraid of something that turned out fine.

A reader may not know who Nathan and Toby are. The writer should use details to help the reader understand.

Some sentences run together. The writer should use end marks correctly.

I was afraid to ride horses myself. I got really scared a few years ago. When they bite you you know it.

I went to watch Nathan at his riding lesson. I was standing behind the fence. I really wanted to ride too. My brother looked like he was having fun.

The riding teacher knew I was afraid of horses already. Then no one was around. I asked how you could get to like horses if you were afraid of them. She put us on Toby. She held on to Toby I held the rope we liked him to the fence. He looked pretty big I knew I had to try. It wasn't easy.

I went a few more times with Nathan. I walked Toby around the barnyard holding onto the rope. Finally I said I would sit on him. It worked out OK.

Name _____ Date _____

Written Composition: Expository

LOOK

Look at the picture in the box below.

THINK

Teachers sometimes take students on field trips to visit interesting places. What makes a field trip interesting? Think of a place that would be a good setting for a field trip.

> **Tip**
>
> List some reasons that explain why that place would be good for a field trip.

WRITE

Write a one-page expository composition that explains why the place you chose would be good for a field trip.

As you write your composition, remember to —

❑ tell why this place would be good for a field trip.

❑ organize ideas in order and use transitions.

❑ develop ideas using facts and examples.

❑ use correct spelling, punctuation, grammar.

❑ make sure your composition is only one page.

> **Tip**
>
> Make sure to use details that support your central idea.

81

Sample Response: Expository

> **Write a one-page expository composition that explains why the place you chose would be good for a field trip.**

The writer sets up a central idea in the topic sentence.

I think a redwood forest would be a good place for a field trip. Redwoods are very unusual trees.

What is so unusual about a redwood? Well redwoods are the tallest trees. They can be as tall as a tall building! When you look up, you sometimes can't see the top of the trees.

Redwoods are also pretty tough. They have thick bark so insects can't bite them. Also, fires cant burn them. There is not enough light for plants to grow near the bottom of a redwood tree. This means fires don't usually burn in a redwood forest.

The writer provides a strong concluding statement.

So, a field trip to a redwood forest would bebe good for our class to learn more about this special tree.

Sample Response: Expository

> Write a one-page expository composition that explains why the place you chose would be good for a field trip.

Whales are the most amazing animels! I want to know more about them. Our class could visit a whale museum on a field trip.

The writer does not support the main idea with explanations. →

I read a book about whales. they live in two different places. In the winter, they eat all the time and get fat. In the summer they don't eat at all. But its OK because they don't need too. Whales swim very far all the time.

Whales can talk to each other. It's not words. It is sounds. I heard it one time on TV. It sounds like wissling and clicking. The guy on TV said whales sing but it didn't sound like singing

The writer ends the composition without a concluding statement. →

to me! I also saw a skeleton of a whale.

Grade 3: Expository

Written Composition: Expository

READ

Read the text in the box below.

> Maria has a pen pal in England named Paul. She is trying to explain to Paul some things about her school. Her favorite activity at school is the class play. She wants to explain to Paul how to put on a class play.

THINK

Think about the activity you enjoy most at school. Then think about how you would explain this activity to a friend.

Tip

Before you begin writing, list the steps needed to do your favorite activity at school.

WRITE

Write a one-page expository composition to explain your favorite activity at school to a friend.

As you write your composition, remember to —

❏ think about this central idea—explaining your favorite activity at school.

❏ organize your ideas, in an order that makes sense, and connect them using transitions.

❏ develop your ideas using facts, details, and explanations.

❏ use correct spelling, capitalization, punctuation, grammar, and sentences.

❏ make sure your composition is not longer than one page.

Tip

Make sure that your topic sentence introduces the central idea and that you have a strong concluding statement.

Name _____ Date _____

Written Composition: Personal Narrative

TEKS 3.17B, 3.17C, 3.17D, 3.19

READ

Read the story in the box below.

> Tanya already had two older brothers. She loved them, but she really wanted a sister. Then one day her mom gave Tanya good news. She was having a new baby. After little Latrice was born, Tanya was very happy. She would have someone to share things with, things her brothers cared nothing about. Having a baby sister changed Tanya's life for the better.

THINK

Think of a time when something good happened to you. Then think about how it made your life better.

WRITE

Write a one-page personal narrative about something that happened that made your life better.

As you write your composition, remember to —

❏ describe a personal experience—an event that made your life better.

❏ organize your ideas, and connect them using transitions.

❏ develop your ideas with details that will help the reader understand your experience and your feelings.

❏ use correct spelling, capitalization, punctuation, grammar, and sentences.

❏ make sure your composition is not longer than one page.

Written Composition:
Personal Narrative

LOOK

Look at the picture in the box below.

THINK

The summer is a great time to have an adventure.

Think about an adventure you enjoyed over the summer.
Then think about what happened during this adventure.

WRITE

Write a one-page personal narrative about your adventure.

As you write your composition, remember to —

❏ describe your summer adventure.

❏ organize ideas in order and use transitions.

❏ develop your ideas with details and feelings.

❏ use correct spelling, punctuation, and grammar.

❏ make sure your composition is just one page.

Written Composition: Expository

TEKS 3.17B, 3.17C, 3.17D, 3.20A(i), 3.20A(ii), 3.20A(iii)

READ

Read the text in the box below.

> Jacob believes that science is the most important subject at school. He plans to be a doctor some day. He thinks that science will help us find cures for many diseases. He cannot think of anything more important than that.

THINK

Think about the subject at school that you think is most important. Why do you think this subject is so important?

WRITE

Write a one-page expository composition to explain why the school subject you chose is the most important.

As you write your composition, remember to —

❑ think about a central idea—why you think a certain school subject is the most important at school.

❑ organize your ideas, and connect them using transitions.

❑ develop your ideas using facts, details, and explanations to support your central idea.

❑ use correct spelling, capitalization, punctuation, grammar, and sentences.

❑ make sure your composition is not longer than one page.

89

Written Composition: Expository

LOOK

Look at the picture in the box below.

THINK

Some animals make wonderful class pets. Think about an animal that would make the best class pet. Why would you choose that animal?

WRITE

Write a one-page expository composition that explains why the animal you chose would be the best class pet.

As you write your composition, remember to —

❏ think about a central idea—why the animal you chose would be the best class pet.

❏ organize your ideas, and connect them using transitions.

❏ develop your ideas using facts, details, and explanations to support your central idea.

❏ use correct spelling, capitalization, punctuation, grammar, and sentences.

❏ make sure your composition is not longer than one page.

Name _____ Date _____

Revising

After you have finished the first draft of a composition, your next step is **revising**. Revising means fixing problems to improve your writing. There may be parts that do not make sense or ideas that are out of order. Revising includes adding, deleting, and moving text.

When you revise your composition, you can delete text that you do not need. You can add or move text to help the reader better understand your ideas. You can also make sure that you have used a variety of sentences and that you have written with the audience in mind.

Read this chart to learn more about ways to revise your writing.

Check
• Make sure your main idea is clear by including a topic sentence.
• Make sure all of the examples, facts, and details you used help the reader understand your main idea.
• Make sure you have a strong concluding statement.
Add
• Add transition words, such as *but, then*, and *for example* to connect ideas.
Delete
• Delete words, sentences, and paragraphs that are not about the main idea.
• Delete facts that do not give information about the main idea, even if they are interesting.
Move
• Move a word, sentence, or paragraph if it would fit better in another part of the paper.
Sentences
• Use a variety of simple and compound sentences.
• When possible, combine sentences that have the same ideas into one sentence.

Name _____ Date _____

Revising

Read the introduction and the passage below. Then read each question.
Fill in the circle of the correct answer.

Jack started writing this composition about keeping pets safe. He needs help revising it. Read the paper and think about the changes he should make. Then answer the questions that follow.

Protecting Pets

(1) When a storm comes, people might have to leave their homes quickly. (2) Pets may get left behind. (3) The pets may face danger from floods. (4) The pets may need to find higher ground. (5) Pets may not have enough food to eat. (6) Pets face great danger in emergencies.

(7) This is especially true when there is a hurricane. (8) Some hurricanes may cause damage in the places they hit. (9) Many trees may be pulled out of the ground.

(10) In the days after a hurricane, volunteers join in the cleanup. (11) Some help find lost pets. (12) Pets need lots of exercise. (13) Thanks to many volunteers, many pets are saved each year.

(14) It is very important to have a disaster plan for pets. (15) Do you have a plan for your pets?

> **Tip**
>
> When short sentences have the same subject, you can combine them into one sentence by forming a compound predicate. Think about how to combine them.

> **Tip**
>
> If a detail does not belong, you should delete it.

Grade 3: Revising

© Houghton Mifflin Harcourt Publishing Company

Name _____ Date _____

1 Which is the **BEST** way to combine sentences 3 and 4?

- ⬭ The pets may face danger from floods and may need to find higher ground.

- ⬭ The pets may face danger from floods they may need to find higher ground.

- ⬭ The pets may face danger from floods, and the pets they may need to find higher ground.

- ⬭ The pets may face danger from floods, may need to find higher ground.

TEKS 3.17C

2 Which transition word should be added to the beginning of sentence 5?

- ⬭ Also

- ⬭ Before

- ⬭ First

- ⬭ Because

TEKS 3.17C

3 Where should sentence 6 move to make more sense in this paper?

- ⬭ Before sentence 1

- ⬭ Before sentence 3

- ⬭ Before sentence 4

- ⬭ Before sentence 5

TEKS 3.17C

Tip
The topic sentence gives the main idea of a paragraph. Where would be the best place to put a topic sentence?

GO ON ➤

Grade 3: Revising

4 Which sentence could **BEST** be added after sentence 8?

- ○ Hurricanes gather energy through contact with warm ocean waters.

- ○ After a strong storm, homes can be destroyed.

- ○ Pilots called Hurricane Hunters fly into these storms to study them.

- ○ Today, people are more aware of the dangers of storms.

TEKS 3.20A(ii)

Tip

Reread the whole paragraph. Which sentence gives an important detail about the main idea?

5 Which sentence does **NOT** belong in the third paragraph?

- ○ Sentence 10

- ○ Sentence 11

- ○ Sentence 12

- ○ Sentence 13

TEKS 3.17C

6 Which sentence could **BEST** be added after sentence 15?

- ○ You may want to keep a flashlight nearby in case the electricity goes out.

- ○ Pets are good for people because they help people stay happy and healthy.

- ○ When you know a hurricane is coming, stock supplies such as food and water.

- ○ By planning for an emergency, you can help keep your pets safe and healthy.

TEKS 3.20A(iii)

Tip

Look for the sentence that sums up the main idea of the composition.

**Read the introduction and the passage below. Then read each question.
Fill in the circle of the correct answer.**

Mai started writing this story about a club she started. Read Mai's story and look for ways she can revise and improve her writing. Then answer the questions that follow.

The Kite Society

(1) First we made a list of fun things we enjoy doing together. (2) Then we voted on what kind of club we would start. (3) Now we're the members of our very own kite-flying club! (4) We call our club the Kite Society. (5) Once my brother was in a club. (6) My friends and I decided to start a club last summer.

(7) At first, there were only three of us in the Kite Society. (8) Each week my parents would walk with us from school to the park to fly kites together. (9) We wanted more students to join us. (10) We hung posters at school.

(11) Soon the Kite Society had ten members. (12) We had twenty members. (13) Now we have thirty members! (14) We decided we should have officers for our club. (15) I was elected president.

(16) We still meet every week to fly kites together. (17) Sometimes we have contests to see who can fly their kites the highest. (18) My kite is red and blue. (19) We even work together to pick up litter in the park. (20) I'm already thinking of new clubs I would like to start.

GO ON

1 Which sentence does **NOT** belong in the first paragraph?

- ⬭ Sentence 2
- ⬭ Sentence 3
- ⬭ Sentence 4
- ⬭ Sentence 5

TEKS 3.17C

2 Where should sentence 6 move to make more sense in this story?

- ⬭ Before sentence 1
- ⬭ Before sentence 2
- ⬭ Before sentence 3
- ⬭ No revision is needed.

TEKS 3.17C

3 Which sentence could **BEST** be added after sentence 8?

- ⬭ Walking is good exercise.
- ⬭ My parents are both teachers.
- ⬭ It was so much fun!
- ⬭ I love to walk in the park!

TEKS 3.17C

4 Which is the **BEST** way to combine sentences 9 and 10?

- ⬭ We wanted more students to join us, hung posters at school.
- ⬭ We wanted more students to join us, so we hung posters at school.
- ⬭ We wanted more students to join us, but we hung posters at school.
- ⬭ We wanted more students to join us to hang posters at school.

TEKS 3.17C

Name _____ Date _____

5 Which transition word should be added to the beginning of sentence 12?

○ First

○ Then

○ Because

○ Finally

TEKS 3.17C

6 Which is the **BEST** way to combine sentences 14 and 15?

○ We decided we should have officers for our club, but I was elected president.

○ We decided we should have officers for our club, or I was elected president.

○ We decided we should have officers for our club, I was elected president.

○ We decided we should have officers for our club, and I was elected president.

TEKS 3.17C

7 Which sentence does **NOT** belong in the last paragraph?

○ Sentence 16

○ Sentence 17

○ Sentence 18

○ Sentence 19

TEKS 3.17C

8 Which sentence could **BEST** be added after sentence 19?

○ I enjoy being part of a club.

○ The town is building a new park.

○ This work is very boring.

○ I don't know why people litter.

TEKS 3.17C

> **Read the introduction and the passage below. Then read each question.**
> **Fill in the circle of the correct answer.**

Jesse started writing this report about schoolhouses of 200 years ago. He needs help revising it. Read the report and think about the changes he should make. Then answer the questions that follow.

Early Classrooms

(1) Children from the first to the eighth grades were taught their lessons in one classroom. (2) Some one-room schools had as many as 40 students. (3) Others had as few as six. (4) The teacher taught reading, writing, math, history, English, and all other subjects.

(5) The teacher's desk was at the front of the room, facing the children. (6) The youngest children sat near the front. (7) They wore old-fashioned clothes. (8) The oldest children sat in the back. (9) In some schools, the boys sat on one side of the room. (10) The girls sat on the other side of the room.

(11) When the teacher called on students, they stood up and answered the question. (12) There was only one teacher for each schoolhouse. (13) The children who were in the same grade listened to the teacher's lesson. (14) The other children sat quietly. (15) They read their books. (16) I always sit quietly in class.

(17) In the United States, most one-room schoolhouses are no longer used as schools. (18) However, in some small communities, they are still used as schools.

Name _____ Date _____

1 Which topic sentence could **BEST** be added before sentence 1?

- About 200 years ago, most American children went to a one-room schoolhouse.

- President Herbert Hoover once learned his lessons in a one-room schoolhouse.

- About 200 years ago, town meetings and picnics were held in one-room schoolhouses.

- Most of the one-room schoolhouses are gone now.

TEKS 3.20A(i)

2 Which sentence does **NOT** belong in the second paragraph?

- Sentence 5

- Sentence 6

- Sentence 7

- Sentence 8

TEKS 3.17C

3 Which is the **BEST** way to combine sentences 9 and 10?

- In some schools, the boys sat on one side of the room, the girls sitting on the other side.

- In some schools, the boys sat on one side of the room so the girls could sit on the other side.

- In some schools, the boys sat on one side of the room, the girls sat on the other side.

- In some schools, the boys sat on one side of the room, and the girls sat on the other side.

TEKS 3.17C

4 Where should sentence 12 move to make more sense in this paper?

- After sentence 3

- After sentence 8

- After sentence 10

- No revision is needed.

TEKS 3.17C

Grade 3: Revising Practice

5 Which is the **BEST** way to combine sentences 14 and 15?

○ The other children sat quietly, they read their books.

○ The other children sat quietly and read their books.

○ The other children sat quietly, but they read their books.

○ The other children sat quietly, or they read their books.

TEKS 3.17C

6 Which sentence does **NOT** belong in the third paragraph?

○ Sentence 13

○ Sentence 14

○ Sentence 15

○ Sentence 16

TEKS 3.17C

7 Which sentence could **BEST** be added after sentence 17?

○ Some schoolhouses were painted red, but most were white.

○ They have been torn down, or they are used for other purposes.

○ A typical school day was 9 a.m. to 4 p.m.

○ The teacher's house was often attached to the school.

TEKS 3.20A(ii)

8 Which concluding sentence could **BEST** be added after sentence 18?

○ I wouldn't like to learn in a one-room schoolhouse.

○ It would be silly to use one-room schoolhouses in large communities.

○ Schools have changed over time, but one-room schoolhouses served students well 200 years ago.

○ The students who still learn in a one-room schoolhouse are very lucky.

TEKS 3.20A(iii)

Grade 3: Revising Practice

Editing

TEKS 3.17D, 3.22A, 3.22B, 3.22C, 3.23B, 3.23C, 3.24B, 3.24C, 3.24D, 3.24E, 3.24F

Editing

Editing is the next step after revising. When you edit your writing, you read it carefully to look for errors in grammar, punctuation, capitalization, and spelling. The goal of editing is to correct errors that may confuse your readers.

Read the chart to learn more about ways to edit your writing.

Grammar

- Make sure you have used nouns, verbs, adjectives, and adverbs correctly.

- Check that sentences have complete subjects and complete predicates.

- Be sure that simple and compound sentences have correct subject-verb agreement.

Punctuation and Capitalization

- Make sure you use apostrophes correctly in contractions and possessives.

- Check that you have used commas correctly in a series and in dates.

- Be sure to capitalize proper nouns such as the names of people and places. You should also capitalize periods in history and the official titles of people.

Spelling

- Check that you have spelled homophones correctly (*bear/bare, week/weak, road/rode*).

- Check that you have changed *y* to *i* in verbs such as *carry* before adding *-ed*.

- Check that you have spelled words correctly with double consonants in the middle.

Editing

> **Read the introduction and the passage below. Then read each question.**
> **Fill in the circle of the correct answer.**

Anna started writing this story. She needs help editing it. Think about the changes she should make. Then answer the questions that follow.

A Gift for Mrs. Thompson

(1) Jada and Cathy adored there teacher, Mrs. Thompson.

(2) She read stories better than anyone else.

(3) One day, Mrs. Thompson announced that she wouldnt be teaching next year. (4) Jada and Cathy knew they would miss her.

(5) "Let's get a present for her," said Cathy.

(6) Jada and Cathy walked through the highland mall. (7) They look in a food store. (8) They looked in a T-shirt store. (9) They just could not find anything they liked.

(10) The girls was about to give up when they saw a card store. (11) In the back, they saw a statue on a shelf. (12) The statue showed a woman reading to a group of children.

(13) "This is perfect!" cried Jada. (14) "When Mrs. Thompson looks at this statue, teacher will definitely think of us."

Tip
Look for words that sound alike but are spelled differently and have different meanings.

Tip
Make sure that the subject and verb in a sentence agree.

GO ON ➡

Grade 3: Editing

1 What change, if any, should be made in sentence 1?

○ Insert a comma after *adored*

○ Change *there* to **their**

○ Change *teacher* to **teecher**

○ Make no change

TEKS 3.24E

2 What change, if any, should be made in sentence 3?

○ Change *announced* to **announces**

○ Change *wouldnt* to **wouldn't**

○ Delete *be*

○ Make no change

TEKS 3.24F

Tip
Think about what punctuation mark belongs in a contraction.

3 What change should be made in sentence 6?

○ Insert a comma after *Cathy*

○ Change *searched* to **searches**

○ Change *through* to **threw**

○ Change *highland mall* to **Highland Mall**

TEKS 3.23B(i)

Tip
Use capital letters for the name of a specific place.

4 What change should be made in sentence 7?

○ Change *they* to **she**

○ Change *look* to **looked**

○ Change *a* to **an**

○ Change *food store* to **Food Store**

TEKS 3.22A(i)

5 What change, if any, should be made in sentence 10?

○ Change *was* to **were**

○ Insert a comma after *up*

○ Change *card store* to **Card Store**

○ Make no change

TEKS 3.22C

6 What change should be made in sentence 14?

○ Change *at* to **on**

○ Delete the comma after *statue*

○ Insert **our** before *teacher*

○ Change *definitely* to **definite**

TEKS 3.22B

Tip
Make sure that a sentence has a complete subject.

Editing
PRACTICE

TEKS 3.17D, 3.22A(ii),
3.22A(iii), 3.22A(iv),
3.23B(iii), 3.23C(ii),
3.24B(iii), 3.24B(iv)

**Read the introduction and the passage below. Then read each question.
Fill in the circle of the correct answer.**

---

*Luis started writing this report about Lady Bird Johnson. Read Luis's report
and look for ways he can correct and improve it. Then answer the questions
that follow.*

Lady Bird Johnson

(1) The first lady of our nation works very hard. (2) She and her husband,
the president, try to make a America we can all be proud of. (3) Lady Bird
Johnson was the first lady of the United States from 1963 until 1969. (4) A
first lady is the wife of the president. (5) Lady Bird Johnson was married to
president Lyndon B. Johnson.

(6) What did Lady Bird Johnson hope to do! (7) She hoped to make
our country more beautiful, and she started her work at the White House.
(8) She worked with people to plant gardens and flowers. (9) She continued
planting all over Washington, D.C. (10) She wanted to make the city more
beautiful for both adults and childs. (11) Everyone was quickly pleased with
her work.

(12) The first lady also formed a group to remove liter and plant millions of
flowers and plants all over the country. (13) She said, "Where flowers bloom,
so does hope." (14) Her work made people smile. (15) They enjoyed living
in prettyer cities.

(16) Mrs. Johnson won many awards for her work. (17) The beauty she
helped spread is enjoyed by Americans all over the country today. (18) She
died on July 11 2007, but her good works live on for us to treasure.

Grade 3: Editing Practice

Editing
PRACTICE

TEKS 3.17D, 3.22A(ii),
3.22A(iii), 3.22A(iv),
3.23B(iii), 3.23C(ii),
3.24B(iii), 3.24B(iv)

1 What change, if any, should be made in sentence 2?

○ Change *She* to **Her**

○ Change *try* to **tries**

○ Change *a* to **an**

○ Make no change

TEKS 3.22A(iii)

2 What change, if any, should be made in sentence 5?

○ Change *was* to **were**

○ Change *president* to **President**

○ Insert a comma after *president*

○ Make no change

TEKS 3.23B(iii)

3 What change, if any, should be made in sentence 6?

○ Change *did* to **does**

○ Change *do* to **due**

○ Change *!* to **?**

○ Make no change

TEKS 3.17D

4 What change should be made in sentence 10?

○ Change *wanted* to **wants**

○ Delete *to*

○ Change *beautiful* to **beautifully**

○ Change *childs* to **children**

TEKS 3.22A(ii)

Editing

PRACTICE

TEKS 3.17D, 3.22A(ii),
3.22A(iii), 3.22A(iv),
3.23B(iii), 3.23C(ii),
3.24B(iii), 3.24B(iv)

Name _____ Date _____

5 What change, if any, should be made in sentence 11?

- ⬭ Change *was* to **is**

- ⬭ Change *quickly* to **quick**

- ⬭ Change *her* to **hers**

- ⬭ Make no change

TEKS 3.22A(iv)

6 What change should be made in sentence 12?

- ⬭ Change *a* to **an**

- ⬭ Change *liter* to **litter**

- ⬭ Insert a comma after *liter*

- ⬭ Change *over* to **about**

TEKS 3.24B(iv)

7 What change, if any, should be made in sentence 15?

- ⬭ Change *They* to **Theirs**

- ⬭ Change *prettyer* to **prettier**

- ⬭ Change *cities* to **citys**

- ⬭ Make no change

TEKS 3.24B(iii)

8 What change should be made in sentence 18?

- ⬭ Insert a comma after *July 11*

- ⬭ Delete the comma after *2007*

- ⬭ Change *but* to **or**

- ⬭ Change *for* to **four**

TEKS 3.23C(ii)

107

Editing
PRACTICE

TEKS 3.22A(v), 3.22A(vii),
3.22A(viii), 3.23B(ii),
3.23C(i), 3.23C(ii),
3.24C, 3.24D

> **Read the introduction and the passage below. Then read each question.**
> **Fill in the circle of the correct answer.**

Stephanie started writing this report about a field trip to the Texas Capitol building. Read Stephanie's report and look for ways she can correct and improve it. Then answer the questions that follow.

The Texas Capitol

(1) My class just returned from a field trip to the Texas Capitol building. (2) The building is located in Austin, Texas. (3) It was built in 1888 and still stands as a symbol of pride in the Lone Star State. (4) It is the largest capitol building in the United States!

(5) Did you know that Texans once argued over which city should be the capital? (6) On 1843, some people wanted Houston to be the capital of Texas. (7) They sent men to steal the government's records from Austin.

(8) The thieves almost got away with it! (9) But a woman named Angelina Eberly was watching and caught them in the act. (10) She saw the thieves ran to the street and fired a big cannon. (11) The suden noise from the cannon scared the thieves off!

(12) Eberlys quick thinking had saved the day. (13) The people of Austin got the records back, but Austin remains the capital of Texas to this day.

(14) Angelina Eberly is a hero in Texas. (15) There is even a large statue of her in down town Austin. (16) However, both the Texas Capitol and Eberly's statue are sights you will want to see in Austin.

1 What change, if any, should be made in sentence 3?

- ⬭ Change *built* to **build**
- ⬭ Change *symbol* to **simbol**
- ⬭ Change *Lone Star State* to **lone star state**
- ⬭ Make no change

TEKS 3.23B(ii)

2 What change, if any, should be made in sentence 6?

- ⬭ Change *On* to **In**
- ⬭ Change *wanted* to **want**
- ⬭ Delete *be*
- ⬭ Make no change

TEKS 3.22A(v)

3 What change should be made in sentence 10?

- ⬭ Change *saw* to **sees**
- ⬭ Change *thieves* to **thieve's**
- ⬭ Insert commas after *thieves* and *street*
- ⬭ Change *cannon* to **canon**

TEKS 3.23C(ii)

4 What change, if any, should be made in sentence 11?

- ⬭ Change *suden* to **sudden**
- ⬭ Change *from* to **on**
- ⬭ Delete *off*
- ⬭ Make no change

TEKS 3.24D

GO ON

Editing
PRACTICE

TEKS 3.22A(v), 3.22A(vii),
3.22A(viii), 3.23B(ii),
3.23C(i), 3.23C(ii),
3.24C, 3.24D

5 What change, if any, should be made in sentence 12?

    ⬭ Change *Eberlys* to **Eberly's**

    ⬭ Change *quick* to **quik**

    ⬭ Change *had* to **has**

    ⬭ Make no change

TEKS 3.23C(i)

6 What change should be made in sentence 13?

    ⬭ Change *records* to **record's**

    ⬭ Delete the comma after *back*

    ⬭ Change *but* to **and**

    ⬭ Change *capital* to **Capital**

TEKS 3.22A(vii)

7 What change, if any, should be made in sentence 15?

    ⬭ Change *There* to **They're**

    ⬭ Change *her* to **her's**

    ⬭ Change *down town* to **downtown**

    ⬭ Make no change

TEKS 3.24C

8 What change should be made in sentence 16?

    ⬭ Delete the comma after *However*

    ⬭ Change *However* to **To sum up**

    ⬭ Change *Capitol* to **capitol**

    ⬭ Change *see* to **sea**

TEKS 3.22A(viii)

Grade 3: Editing Practice

Texas Write Source

Assessments

Pretest

Part 1: Basic Elements of Writing

> **Questions 1–10: Read each sentence. Choose the best way to write the underlined part of the sentence. Fill in the circle of the correct answer.**

1 Some birds fly south <u>on</u> the winter.

- ⬭ at
- ⬭ into
- ⬭ for
- ⬭ Make no change

2 Other birds <u>stays</u> in the same place all year.

- ⬭ staying
- ⬭ stay
- ⬭ stayed
- ⬭ Make no change

3 Two bluebirds made a nest for <u>their</u> eggs.

- ⬭ it's
- ⬭ theirs
- ⬭ its
- ⬭ Make no change

4 That bird <u>have</u> a nest under the deck.

- ⬭ has
- ⬭ haves
- ⬭ having
- ⬭ Make no change

5 A dead tree is a <u>best</u> place for a nest.

- ⬭ more better
- ⬭ good
- ⬭ goodest
- ⬭ Make no change

6 Two birds working together can make a nest <u>quickly</u>.

- ⬭ quick
- ⬭ quickest
- ⬭ more quicker
- ⬭ Make no change

Name _____ Date _____

7 The <u>Robin</u> has light blue eggs.

- ○ robin
- ○ Robins
- ○ robins
- ○ Make no change

8 Last spring, a robin <u>builded</u> a nest on our porch.

- ○ is building
- ○ build
- ○ built
- ○ Make no change

9 We <u>did seen</u> many birds at our house this year.

- ○ are seen
- ○ have seen
- ○ has saw
- ○ Make no change

10 Many baby birds eat worms, <u>or</u> some eat only insects.

- ○ so
- ○ if
- ○ but
- ○ Make no change

Questions 11–14: Read each question and fill in the circle of the correct answer.

---

11 Which is a complete sentence written correctly?

- ○ Dad gave us some coins to count.
- ○ Always has change jingling in his pockets!
- ○ My dad, my little brother, and me.
- ○ Have enough coins for the bus?

12 Which is the best way to combine these sentences?

> I collect quarters.
>
> The quarters come from different states.

- ○ I collect quarters, and they come from different states.
- ○ I collect quarters, the quarters from different states.
- ○ I collect quarters from different states.
- ○ I collect quarters and come from different states.

13 Which is an exclamatory sentence that should end with an exclamation point?

- ⊂⊃ Make a different pile for each coin

- ⊂⊃ How much do all these coins weigh

- ⊂⊃ I wonder how much these nickels weigh

- ⊂⊃ I can't believe how heavy these coins are

14 What is the complete subject of the following sentence?

> The huge crowd watched the race in the rain.

- ⊂⊃ the race

- ⊂⊃ the huge crowd

- ⊂⊃ the rain

- ⊂⊃ watched the race

Questions 15–16: A student wrote this paragraph about moving. It may need some changes or corrections. Read the paragraph. Then read each question. Fill in the circle of the correct answer.

My Big Move

(1) When I was 5 years old, my family moved from Ohio to Colorado. (2) The first day of driving was exciting. (3) On the second day, we crossed the Mississippi River. (4) Now we were really in the West! (5) Then I slept a lot because everything was so flat. (6) Finally, we saw mountains. (7) Our car climbed and climbed. (8) That night I saw more stars than I'd ever seen before. (9) It was sad to leave Ohio, but our new home state is really beautiful.

15 What type of paragraph is this?

- ⊂⊃ narrative

- ⊂⊃ persuasive

- ⊂⊃ expository

- ⊂⊃ response to literature

16 Which sentence includes a word that shows a conclusion?

- ⊂⊃ sentence 2

- ⊂⊃ sentence 3

- ⊂⊃ sentence 4

- ⊂⊃ sentence 5

GO ON

Name _____ Date _____

Part 2: Proofreading and Editing

Questions 17–24: Read the passages. Choose the best way to write each underlined part. Fill in the circle of the correct answer.

My favorite place is <u>lake evergreen</u> near my house. My <u>friends</u> and I
                          17   **18**

<u>meat</u> there almost every day. We ride our bikes or float paper boats in the
19

water. Sometimes we get ice cream. Near the lake is the train station. Late

in the afternoon, I go there and wait for my <u>dads'</u> train. Then we walk home
                                              20

together.

17 ○ lake Evergreen

   ○ Lake Evergreen

   ○ "lake evergreen"

   ○ Make no change

19 ○ meet

   ○ mete

   ○ mat

   ○ Make no change

18 ○ frenz

   ○ frends

   ○ freinds

   ○ Make no change

20 ○ dad's

   ○ dads's

   ○ dads

   ○ Make no change

GO ON →

Name _____ Date _____

August 23 2010,
21

Dear Terrell,

We're having a great time in <u>Boston!</u> Yesterday we went on a
22

whale watch. Today we walked on the Freedom Trail, watched jugglers, and

ate fried clams. Tomorrow <u>me and my uncle</u> are going to Truro Beach. He
23

said, <u>It's the best beach in the world!</u> I can't wait to swim in the ocean! You
24

would love it here.

Your buddy,

Ramon

21 ⬭ August, 23, 2010
    ⬭ August 23, 2010
    ⬭ August 23 2010
    ⬭ Make no change

22 ⬭ Boston:
    ⬭ Boston?
    ⬭ Boston,
    ⬭ Make no change

23 ⬭ Me and my Uncle
    ⬭ my uncle and me
    ⬭ my uncle and I
    ⬭ Make no change

24 ⬭ "It's the best beach in the world!"
    ⬭ 'It's the best beach in the world!'
    ⬭ (It's the best beach in the world!)
    ⬭ Make no change

GO ON

Name _____ Date _____

Part 3: Writing   Narrative

READ

You can travel many places. Some places are far away and others
are in your neighborhood.

THINK

What places have you visited? Where have you traveled? Have you traveled
to a place that is far away? Do you travel to places close to your house?
Where is your favorite place to go?

Think of the day when you traveled to your favorite place. Where did you go?
How did you get there? What did you do?

WRITE

Write a narrative composition telling about a day when you traveled
to your favorite place.

As you write your composition, remember to —

❏ focus on one experience—a day that you traveled to your favorite place

❏ organize your ideas in an order that makes sense, and connect those
   ideas using transitions

❏ develop your ideas with specific details

❏ make sure your composition is no longer than one page

Progress Test 1

Part 1: Basic Elements of Writing

> **Questions 1–10: Read each sentence. Choose the best way to write the underlined part of the sentence. Fill in the circle of the correct answer.**

1 Every day after school, Rosa <u>playing</u> kickball.

- ⬭ play
- ⬭ plays
- ⬭ is played
- ⬭ Make no change

2 Rosa and her friends <u>loves</u> to play together.

- ⬭ loving
- ⬭ is loved
- ⬭ love
- ⬭ Make no change

3 She is the <u>faster</u> runner in third grade.

- ⬭ fast
- ⬭ most fast
- ⬭ fastest
- ⬭ Make no change

4 Rosa's team <u>usually</u> wins the game.

- ⬭ most usual
- ⬭ usual
- ⬭ usualler
- ⬭ Make no change

5 Everyone wants to be <u>along her team</u> because she's so good.

- ⬭ on her team.
- ⬭ near her team.
- ⬭ for her team.
- ⬭ Make no change

6 Suddenly, a new boy <u>shown</u> up.

- ⬭ shows
- ⬭ show
- ⬭ showing
- ⬭ Make no change

Name _____ Date _____

7 Omar's not very tall, <u>so</u> he can really kick the ball.

- ⊂⊃ and
- ⊂⊃ but
- ⊂⊃ if
- ⊂⊃ Make no change

9 Kickball games <u>is</u> really fun.

- ⊂⊃ are
- ⊂⊃ was
- ⊂⊃ being
- ⊂⊃ Make no change

8 They all want to be on <u>he's</u> team now.

- ⊂⊃ They're
- ⊂⊃ his
- ⊂⊃ his'
- ⊂⊃ Make no change

10 The <u>child</u> cheer loudly.

- ⊂⊃ Child
- ⊂⊃ childs
- ⊂⊃ children
- ⊂⊃ Make no change

Questions 11–14: Read each question and fill in the circle of the correct answer.

---

11 Which is a complete sentence written correctly?

- ⊂⊃ The Mexican flag is green, white, and red.
- ⊂⊃ The peaceful rule of the Mayas.
- ⊂⊃ After Mayan rule ended in the 1500s.
- ⊂⊃ Ride donkeys through the mountains.

12 Which is the best way to combine these sentences?

> Mexicans farmers grow squash and corn.
>
> Mexican farmers grow beans, too.

- ⊂⊃ Mexicans farmers grow squash and corn, and they grow beans, too.
- ⊂⊃ Mexicans farmers grow squash and corn, and beans, too.
- ⊂⊃ Squash and corn and beans are grown by Mexican farmers.
- ⊂⊃ Mexican farmers grow squash, corn, and beans.

GO ON ➡

Name _____ Date _____

13 Which is an interrogative sentence that should end with a question mark?

- ⬭ Which crops are grown together
- ⬭ How green those plants are
- ⬭ The beans climb up the corn plants
- ⬭ Squash leaves give shade for the roots

14 What is the complete predicate of the following sentence?

> The girl with the red hat kicked the ball.

- ⬭ the girl
- ⬭ the girl with the red hat
- ⬭ the red hat
- ⬭ kicked the ball

Questions 15–16: A student wrote this paragraph about doing laundry. It may need some changes or corrections. Read the paragraph. Then read each question. Fill in the circle of the correct answer.

Doing Laundry

(1) Doing laundry is easy. (2) First, sort the clothes into colors and whites. (3) Then take out everything that should be washed by hand. (4) Measure soap into the washing machine. (5) Choose the cycle. (6) Press the start button. (7) When the wash is done, hang the clothes outside. (8) Finally, fold the dry clothes and put them away.

15 What type of paragraph is this?

- ⬭ descriptive
- ⬭ response to literature
- ⬭ expository
- ⬭ narrative

16 Which sentence includes a word that tells when something should happen?

- ⬭ sentence 2
- ⬭ sentence 4
- ⬭ sentence 5
- ⬭ sentence 6

Name _____ Date _____

Part 2: Proofreading and Editing

Questions 17–24: Read the passages. Choose the best way to write each underlined part. Fill in the circle of the correct answer.

Northern Canada is a very cold place. When I think of Northern Canada,

I think of the ice age! For at least 10,000 years, the Inuit people have lived,
      <u>**17**</u>

hunted, and fished there. Some live in igloos made of ice and snow. In

the summer, <u>them</u> hunt for seals and whales. Some people carve wooden
      18

eagles, <u>witch</u> help to <u>protect</u> them.
   19   **20**

17 ○ Ice Age

    ○ Ice age

    ○ ice Age

    ○ Make no change

19 ○ which

    ○ watch

    ○ what

    ○ Make no change

18 ○ him

    ○ we

    ○ they

    ○ Make no change

20 ○ pratect

    ○ pretect

    ○ proteck

    ○ Make no change

Name _____ Date _____

November 10, 2011

Dear Aunt Tiana,

Thank you so much for my birthday party. My friend Ron

said, <u>It was awesome!</u> The <u>food, music, and decorations</u> were great! Thanks
      21   **22**

for the movie passes, too. <u>We'are</u> going to the movies on Thursday. You are
                      23

the best <u>aunt,</u>
    24

                                Love,

                                Hannah

21 ⬭ (It was awesome!)

    ⬭ 'It was awesome!'

    ⬭ "It was awesome!"

    ⬭ Make no change

23 ⬭ We're

    ⬭ We re

    ⬭ We-re

    ⬭ Make no change

22 ⬭ food, music, and decorations,

    ⬭ food and music and decorations

    ⬭ food music and decorations

    ⬭ Make no change

24 ⬭ the best aunt?

    ⬭ the best aunt!

    ⬭ the best aunt—

    ⬭ Make no change

GO ON ➡

Name _____ Date _____

Part 3: Writing   Expository

READ

When kids go to school, they get there many different ways.

THINK

How do you get to school each day? You may walk, ride in a car, or take a bus.

WRITE

Write an expository composition that explains how you get to school each day.

As you write your composition, remember to —

❏ think about a central idea—how you get to school each day

❏ organize your ideas in an order that makes sense, and connect those ideas using transitions

❏ develop your ideas using facts, details, and experiences

❏ make sure your composition is no longer than one page

STOP

Name _____   Date _____

Progress Test 2
Part 1: Basic Elements of Writing

> **Questions 1–10:** Read each sentence. Choose the best way to write the underlined part of the sentence. Fill in the circle of the correct answer.

1 Mr. Cross and his son sell lobsters at they store.

- ○ their
- ○ they're
- ○ them
- ○ Make no change

2 A lobster has a hard shell but two eyes.

- ○ also
- ○ or
- ○ and
- ○ Make no change

3 Mr. Cross steered his boat on the rock.

- ○ over the rock.
- ○ around the rock.
- ○ through the rock.
- ○ Make no change

4 Lobsters move slow along the sea bottom.

- ○ slowing
- ○ slowed
- ○ slowly
- ○ Make no change

5 Boiling are the best way to cook crabs and lobsters.

- ○ be
- ○ is
- ○ were
- ○ Make no change

6 Lobsters from Maine are larger than lobsters from Florida.

- ○ large
- ○ largely
- ○ largest
- ○ Make no change

GO ON ➡

Name _____ Date _____

7 In New England, people <u>uses</u> traps to catch crabs.

- ⊂⊃ use
- ⊂⊃ using
- ⊂⊃ is using
- ⊂⊃ Make no change

8 Crabs that are too small must be <u>thrown</u> back.

- ⊂⊃ throwed
- ⊂⊃ threw
- ⊂⊃ throw
- ⊂⊃ Make no change

9 How many crabs did you <u>catched</u> today?

- ⊂⊃ catch
- ⊂⊃ catches
- ⊂⊃ caught
- ⊂⊃ Make no change

10 The restaurant called <u>Marley's Fishing Dock</u> is always busy.

- ⊂⊃ marley's fishing dock
- ⊂⊃ Marley's fishing dock
- ⊂⊃ Marley's fishing Dock
- ⊂⊃ Make no change

Questions 11–14: Read each question and fill in the circle of the correct answer.

---

11 Which is a complete sentence written correctly?

- ⊂⊃ Claudia, my aunt.
- ⊂⊃ She is going to marry Brandon.
- ⊂⊃ Are getting married in a church.
- ⊂⊃ Will go to my cousin's house afterward.

12 Which is an exclamatory sentence that should end with an exclamation point?

- ⊂⊃ What a huge cake
- ⊂⊃ Where does he come from
- ⊂⊃ I wonder when they'll cut the cake
- ⊂⊃ It's a little noisy in here

GO ON ➡

Name _____ Date _____

13 Which is the best way to combine these sentences?

> Grandpa danced at the wedding.
>
> Grandpa sang at the wedding, too.

- ⬭ Grandpa danced at the wedding and sang, too.
- ⬭ Grandpa danced and sang at the wedding, too.
- ⬭ Grandpa danced and sang at the wedding.
- ⬭ Grandpa danced at the wedding, and Grandpa sang.

14 What is the complete subject of the following sentence?

> The band began to play as soon as we got to the hall.

- ⬭ the band began to play
- ⬭ the band
- ⬭ began to play as soon
- ⬭ we got to the hall

Questions 15–16: A student wrote this paragraph about the Cherokee people. It may need some changes or corrections. Read the paragraph. Then read each question. Fill in the circle of the correct answer.

---

(1) Many Cherokee people now live in Oklahoma, but they did not always live there. (2) Once they lived in western Georgia. (3) They had roads, schools, and churches. (4) In 1838, the Cherokee were forced to leave their native lands. (5) They had to travel far to the west. (6) Their journey became known as the "Trail of Tears."

15 What type of paragraph is this?

- ⬭ narrative
- ⬭ response to literature
- ⬭ expository
- ⬭ persuasive

16 Which detail sentence could best be added between sentences 5 and 6?

- ⬭ About 4,000 Cherokee died along the way.
- ⬭ Georgia is located on the Atlantic Ocean.
- ⬭ Utah and Wyoming are two Western states.
- ⬭ Many people left Oklahoma in the 1930s.

GO ON ➡

Name _____ Date _____

Part 2: Proofreading and Editing

> **Questions 17–24: Read the passages. Choose the best way to write each underlined part. Fill in the circle of the correct answer.**

Making Compost

Compost is good "food" for your garden. My dad and I make compost at

our home in <u>austin, Texas</u>. Making compost is simple. Start with a pile of dry
        17

leaves. Put them in a barrel with <u>wholes</u> in it. Add some vegetable scraps
                                   18

and grass, and throw in a little dirt. Add more scraps, grass, and dirt each

week until the barrel is full. Pour some water on it every week. <u>Sooner,</u> you'll
                                                                   19

have rich, black compost to feed your plants. My dad says, <u>Every gardener</u>
                                                            20

<u>should have a compost pile.</u>

17 ○ Austin, Texas

  ○ austin, texas

  ○ Austin, texas

  ○ Make no change

18 ○ whole

  ○ halls

  ○ holes

  ○ Make no change

19 ○ Soonest,

  ○ Soon,

  ○ Soonly,

  ○ Make no change

20 ○ "Every gardener should have a compost pile."

  ○ 'Every gardener should have a compost pile.'

  ○ (Every gardener should have a compost pile.)

  ○ Make no change

Name _____ Date _____

Dear Mrs. Jackson,   August 23, 2010

    We are having a yard sale next <u>Saterday.</u> You are welcome to join
                                  21

the sale if you have anything to <u>sell?</u> We plan to offer all of these things:
                                  22

<u>pots pans, books toys tools,</u> and furniture. If you are interested, bring
          23

your things to the <u>Clarks house</u> on Friday.
              24

                                    Thank you,

                                    Matt Moran

21 ⬯ Satterday

    ⬯ Saturday

    ⬯ Satturday

    ⬯ Make no change

23 ⬯ pots and pans, and books, and toys, and tools,

    ⬯ pots and pans, books and toys, and tools,

    ⬯ pots, pans, books, toys, tools,

    ⬯ Make no change

22 ⬯ sell.

    ⬯ sell,

    ⬯ sell:

    ⬯ Make no change

24 ⬯ Clark's house

    ⬯ Clarks house's

    ⬯ Clarks' house

    ⬯ Make no change

GO ON ➡

Name _____ Date _____

Part 3: Writing   Expository

READ

Winter, Spring, Summer, and Fall

There are four seasons in a year.

THINK

What is your favorite season? Why do you like it?
What is special about your season?

Think about the reasons why you like that season.

WRITE

Write an expository composition explaining what your favorite season is
and why.

As you write your composition, remember to —

❏ think about a central idea—your favorite season

❏ organize your ideas in an order that makes sense, and connect those
ideas using transitions

❏ develop your ideas using facts, details, and reasons

❏ make sure your composition is no longer than one page

Post-test

Part 1: Basic Elements of Writing

Questions 1–10: Read each sentence. Choose the best way to write the underlined part of the sentence. Fill in the circle of the correct answer.

1 Raccoons are <u>smart</u> than most animals.

- ⬭ smartest
- ⬭ smarter
- ⬭ smartly
- ⬭ Make no change

2 A raccoon's tail has either four <u>and</u> five black rings.

- ⬭ but
- ⬭ also
- ⬭ or
- ⬭ Make no change

3 All raccoons <u>has</u> black masks over their faces.

- ⬭ have
- ⬭ is having
- ⬭ having
- ⬭ Make no change

4 They <u>uses</u> their paws like hands.

- ⬭ using
- ⬭ use
- ⬭ are used
- ⬭ Make no change

5 Raccoons <u>can open</u> jars with their paws.

- ⬭ can opening
- ⬭ can opened
- ⬭ are open
- ⬭ Make no change

6 A <u>raccoons</u> eats many different foods.

- ⬭ Raccoons
- ⬭ Raccoon
- ⬭ raccoon
- ⬭ Make no change

Name _____   Date _____

7 I borrowed <u>him</u> book about raccoons.

- ⬭ he's
- ⬭ his
- ⬭ he
- ⬭ Make no change

8 It <u>eated</u> some food from the garbage can.

- ⬭ eating
- ⬭ ated
- ⬭ ate
- ⬭ Make no change

9 Raccoons can see <u>very good</u> at night.

- ⬭ very well
- ⬭ much gooder
- ⬭ really good
- ⬭ Make no change

10 Do more raccoons live <u>off</u> the country or the city?

- ⬭ on
- ⬭ at
- ⬭ in
- ⬭ Make no change

Questions 11–14: Read each question and fill in the circle of the correct answer.

---

11 Which is a complete sentence written correctly?

- ⬭ Her head bending over her hands.
- ⬭ Sitting at a small table by the fire.
- ⬭ Blue, yellow, and purple beads everywhere.
- ⬭ Sharon is making a necklace.

12 Which is the best way to combine these sentences?

> She uses strong thread.
>
> The thread is thin, too.

- ⬭ She uses strong thread that is also thin.
- ⬭ She uses strong thread and thin thread.
- ⬭ She uses strong, thin thread.
- ⬭ She uses strong thread and it's thin.

GO ON ➡

Name _____ Date _____

13 What is the complete predicate of the following sentence?

> The basketball team played a great game on Saturday.

- ⬭ The basketball team
- ⬭ played a great game on Saturday
- ⬭ on Saturday
- ⬭ a great game on Saturday

14 Which is an interrogative sentence that should end with a question mark?

- ⬭ Those beads are made of glass
- ⬭ What a beautiful necklace
- ⬭ The blue and silver beads are pretty
- ⬭ Whose necklace is that

Questions 15–16: A student wrote this paragraph about statues and acid rain. It may need some changes or corrections. Read the paragraph. Then read each question. Fill in the circle of the correct answer.

Why Old Statues Crumble

(1) Have you ever looked at old statues in parks? (2) Many statues are missing noses or fingers, or the shoulders slope. (3) These statues are made of limestone. (4) In the past 50 years, acid rain has become a real problem. (5) It can ruin a statue in a few years.

15 What type of paragraph is this?

- ⬭ expository
- ⬭ response to literature
- ⬭ persuasive
- ⬭ narrative

16 Where could this sentence best be added?

> Limestone can be damaged by acid rain.

- ⬭ between sentences 1 and 2
- ⬭ between sentences 2 and 3
- ⬭ between sentences 3 and 4
- ⬭ between sentences 4 and 5

GO ON ➡

Part 2: Proofreading and Editing

Questions 17–24: Read the passages. Choose the best way to write each underlined part. Fill in the circle of the correct answer.

"May I ask a <u>cuestion</u>, Senator Philips?" said Felipe very politely.
17

"Of course," the Senator said as he stood and <u>weighted</u> on the stage. "Do
18

you support keeping school open all year round?" Felipe asked. "Or do you

think it should be closed for the summer?"

"Well, I can see why you'd want to know <u>that, the</u> Senator
19

chuckled. "<u>I'm</u> pleased to tell you that I think summer should always be a
20

holiday!"

17 ⬭ kweschun

⬭ queschion

⬭ question

⬭ Make no change

18 ⬭ waited

⬭ waitered

⬭ weighed

⬭ Make no change

19 ⬭ that" the

⬭ that the

⬭ that," the

⬭ Make no change

20 ⬭ Im

⬭ I'am

⬭ Im'

⬭ Make no change

GO ON

Name _____ Date _____

<u>October 27, 2010</u>
21

<u>Dear dr Peabody,</u>
22

I want to learn to read and speak the Japanese language. Your son

George says that you wrote a book about Japan, so I thought you might be

able to help. Where should I <u>start.</u> Do you know any teachers? Thank you for
23

any help you can <u>give I.</u>
24

Sincerely,

Anitra (George's friend)

21 ⬭ October 27 2010

    ⬭ October, 27, 2010

    ⬭ October 27 2010,

    ⬭ Make no change

23 ⬭ start?

    ⬭ start,

    ⬭ start!

    ⬭ Make no change

22 ⬭ DR.

    ⬭ Dr.

    ⬭ dr.

    ⬭ Make no change

24 ⬭ give myself

    ⬭ give it

    ⬭ give me

    ⬭ Make no change

Part 3: Writing   Narrative

LOOK

Look at the picture in the box below.

THINK

Think of something fun you have done with a parent or other family member.
Who was with you? What did you do? Why was it fun?

WRITE

Write a narrative composition telling about a day when you did something fun
with a family member.

As you write your composition, remember to —

❏ focus on one experience—something fun you did with a family member

❏ organize your ideas in an order that makes sense, and connect those
   ideas using transitions

❏ develop your ideas with specific details

❏ make sure your composition is no longer than one page